Resilient

*Tools For Getting Up After Life
Knocks You Down*

Dr. Bill Effler

Copyright © 2024

ISBN: 9798880430727

All Rights Reserved. Any unauthorized reprint or use of this material is strictly prohibited. No part of this book may be reproduced or transmitted in any form or by any means, electronic or mechanical, including photocopying, recording, or by any information storage and retrieval system without express written permission from the author.

All reasonable attempts have been made to verify the accuracy of the information provided in this publication. Nevertheless, the author assumes no responsibility for any errors and/or omissions.

The author of this book does not dispense advice or prescribe the use of any technique as a form of treatment for physical, emotional, or medical problems of any kind. The author only intends to offer information to help either the reader, a loved one or, use in a small group setting. All examples or case studies cited are based on forty years of cumulative professional experience; names, gender, places, and other pertinent information has been changed to ensure total anonymity. Any similarities seen by the reader would be total coincidence. In the event any of the information in this book is used by the reader, which is an individual right, the author and publisher assume no responsibility for actions taken.

re·sil·ient
/rəˈzilēənt/

Adjective
also considered an intransitive verb

1. To withstand or recover quickly from difficult conditions.
2. Other considerations: strong, tough, hardy, buoyant, adaptable, flexible, bending, durable, strong, stout, to recoil or spring back into shape.
3. Origin, from Latin in mid 17th century

LATIN

Resilire resilient –
(re-zeel) – leaping back, salio, to jump, recoil.

ENGLISH

resile; to abandon, get back to former position, revert.

FRENCH

resilir -
to recoil
to return to a prior position

4. Other considerations:
resigned, adj (1555) resigning, adj. (1648) resilience, n. (1626) resiliency, adv. (1651)

Though we experience every kind of pressure, we're not crushed. At times we don't know what to do, but quitting is not an option. We are persecuted by others, but God has not forsaken us. We may be knocked down, but not out…We consider living to mean that we are constantly being handed over to death for Jesus' sake so that the life of Jesus will be revealed through our humanity. So, then, death is at work in us but it releases life in you…

Yes, all things work together for your enrichment…For even though our outer person gradually wears out, our inner being is renewed every single day. We view our short-lived trouble in the light of eternity. We see our difficulties as the substance that produces for us eternal, weighty glory far beyond comparison, because we don't focus our attention on what is seen but on what is unseen. For what is seen is temporary, but the unseen realm is eternal.

                        2 Corinthians 4. 8-10 & 16-18
                        The Passion translation

Endorsements

My longtime friend, professor, and mentor does it again. "Resilient: Tools For Getting Up After Life Knocks You Down" by Dr. Bill Effler is a pictorial journey through adversity, recovery, and triumph. As a Licensed Professional Counselor-Supervisor and the CEO of *Clearfork Academy* in Fort Worth Texas, I find Dr. Effler's approach to facing adversity extraordinarily insightful. Considering the epidemic proportions of suicide and mental health dis-ease, his call to the church was profound and necessary: "Every believer needs to better acquaint themselves with tools needed for living with people who are experiencing pain. This is not a call to counselors and pastors alone, but a call to every person who calls themselves a believer in Jesus Christ."

Austin Davis, LPC-S
Founder & CEO of Clearfork Academy
Fort Worth, Texas

"Resilient" … it's more than a buzzword in culture. It is a true desire for so many. In his book, Effler provides a practical approach on how to get back up after having to face and address life's greatest difficulties. His words not only challenge readers but explains how to live resiliently. Those who take this book seriously will find wisdom on every page.

Read it, embrace it, and get back up!

Shannon Chapman
Lead Pastor, City Church of Chattanooga
Chattanooga, Tennessee

Unfair and painful experiences in life are a given. Getting back up after a disappointment *is a choice*. For over twenty years I have seen *resilience* play out in Bill's life. Through his experiences with me as a case counselor in a residential treatment facility in California and continued mentoring over the years (critical to maintaining resilient living), I know Bill to be a person who clearly and practically shares his personal journey, passions, honesty, and down-to-earth counsel with those in deep need. All that Bill shares in *Resilient* represents a lifetime of tested and proven strategies that are a compass that will lead readers to discovering, 'the resilient life'.

Mike Speakman
Mike@MikeSpeakman.com
Phoenix, Arizona

As a therapist and professor, I find this book to be a needed message of hope to anyone who has been knocked down. Discouragement and failure are part of life. Sadly, resilience is a forgotten aspect of the Christian journey that is seldom addressed. In *Resilient, Tools For Getting Up After Life Knocks You Down"*, Dr. Effler vulnerably and brilliantly reminds readers of the function, purpose, and importance of resilience.

Dr. Greg Fischer, PhD, LMFT
Assistant Professor of Clinical Psychology
George Fox University
Newberg, Oregon

Having faced false accusations and jail time while doing humanitarian work in third world countries, I know the trials and sacrifice that await those doing good works. To be clear, resilience looks very different in deeply impoverished settings of the globe as compared to our sanitized, north American way of living. Resiliency in third world countries is mandatory while in the United States, resilience is an afterthought, at best. Effler's *Resilient,* speaks to a variety of settings in life, be it as a missionary, entrepreneur, or stay-at-home mom. Personally, I took Effler's words as a plea to consider tapping more deeply into the power of resiliency and choose to navigate the disappointments in my own life, more intentionally. Effler is a "Mentor of the printed page."

Brian Lindsey
Director/Founder of Missions Life
Cleveland, Tennessee
brian@missionslife.org

Dr Effler has done an amazing job with this book. Following my own "knock down", I have experienced my own personal resilience. I agree with Dr. Effler, "resilience is a "gift from God" available to everyone. No matter how far or how hard a person tries to run from God, God is always there to woo 'the runner' back. Dr. Effler's insights came at just the right time for me and I hope, for every reader.

Brandon Chatfield
Licensed Realtor

Resilience is a needed skill to overcome hardship that each of us will experience. Dr. Effler's teaching, "Starting over is part of the economy of God", is an important truth that hurting people must discover and, experience the hope that comes in the journey of healing. "Resilient, Tools For Getting Up After Life Knocks You Down" gives concrete steps to begin a journey of healing and live a resilient life for the everyday person.

Mark Carpenter, Administrative Director, and staff counselor
The Transformation Center
Chattanooga, Tennessee.

"After helping people over many years step into God's best for their lives, there is one theme I have continued to see: *the power of the past*. When left unresolved, the past is often an anchor that holds people back from all God has for them. But when pain is processed and healing comes, that which was designed to destroy a person, becomes a place of profound healing. I'm so glad Bill has written this book. Out of his own journey, *Resilient* is written in a way that offers help and hope so others can experience healing and experience the restored life that Jesus offers."

Matt Tommey
Artist, Author & Mentor
MattTommeyMentoring.com

In this compelling study, William Effler demonstrates with richness and clarity the necessity for resiliency in all dimensions of human life. As a former pastor and university instructor, Effler asserts that resilience is essential and not an 'add on' in Christian discipleship. Resiliency is of particular importance, particularly in ministering to those from diverse cultures facing difficulties in challenging times. This is a must-read for those experiencing spiritual and psychological battles.

Dr. Rolando Cuellar
Associate Professor of Intercultural Studies
Lee University
Cleveland, Tennessee

Dr. Effler's "Resilient" offers practical tools for overcoming life's difficulties. As an intern clinician who works closely with at-risk youth, "Resilient" has helped me evaluate how resilient my clients are and what changes need to be made in their lives so they can become more resilient. My work with highly 'at risk clients' has been helped as I have drawn upon both the research data and the practicality found in Dr. Effler's writing.

Shannon Riese, Registered Marriage and Family Therapist Intern,
Senior Clinical Services Specialist at x#*7/
Research assistant to Dr. Effler

Dr. Effler has provided a powerful resource in *Resilient, Tools for Getting Up After Life Knocks You Down,* that we have yet to see on a bookshelf. As community leaders that work with people who are deeply at-risk, we have seen, firsthand, the power that resilience plays in salvaging a person's life. In Effler's own words, "Once a person faces their pain, a person will discover the very events that that once brought devastation are now transformed in unimagined ways." *Resilient* offers practical guidance in discerning how to help hurting communities and individual lives. This book will be added to our library and used as a resource to better serve our community.

Jevin and Stephanie Morris
Co-founders and Directors, *Catalyst For the Nations Ministry*
Outreach Coordinators at *Mission 180*
Directors with *Compassion Church*
Hannibal, Missouri

Resilient, is a book not for the faint of heart. Dr. Effler pointedly shares practical guidance, his own personal real-life experiences and case studies that assist his readers in crossing the bridge called, "Life". Written with truth, transparency, and vulnerability Effler's words are a challenge to the world, that the world needs to hear in these troubling times.

Amy Pilgrim
Amypilgrim70@gmail.com
Chattanooga, Tennessee

Gleaning from Dr. Effler's wisdom over the last twelve years, while facing my own unexpected knockdowns of personal loss and trauma, *Resilient* came to me at the perfect time. The practical guidance found in the pages of this book not only helped me frame and better understand my past setbacks but also, speak to my current challenges and equip me to live with a more resiliency in my future.

Rachelle Hopkins
Former Student

Unforeseen hardships of life are a reality. Sadly, life's hardships, whether large or small, impact how we worship an unchanging God. The shepherd-King, David, is one of the greatest examples of resilience found in scripture as he would come to know the power of personal resilience during several dark chapters of his life. Chapter by chapter, Dr. Effler challenges his readers to examine their lives more deeply while offering tools to develop a heart like that of the shepherd-King, David. One proof of the truly resilient life is seen by how a person worships, *especially when experiencing trials*. Sacrificial worship may be one of the greatest gifts a person can offer God and in return, receive a download of added and needed resilience. A life committed to worship is regularly replenished with God-given resilience.

Shane Selby and Makayla McKibben-Selby,
Eleventh Hour Worship
Chattanooga, Tennessee
booking@eleventhhourworship.com

Dr. Effler has been a mentor and friend of mine for nearly 15 years. I am not surprised that the pages of this book are filled with the same practical wisdom that so aptly characterize his life. As an entrepreneur and business owner, I cannot overly exaggerate the critical role resilience plays in the success and longevity of any business enterprise. Effler's thoughts on the role of community as a 'midwife for delivering a person's future' are particularly helpful and thought provoking. I would have never started my own business or experienced success at a young age without the priceless advice I received from an entire community of mentors and dear friends. My current business culture's continued insights, and at times, correction, have guided me in building a highly profitable business that enriches the lives of its employees, provides a valuable service to customers while having, international impact. If you are looking to develop the grit necessary to lead a life of significance, I highly recommend reading, *Resilient*.

Steven Gilliam
Carolina Bearing Company, LLC
Greenville, South Carolina
Smgilliam831@gmail.com

Resilience is more than persistence. Resilience is a pathway for encountering God's personal healing power which in turn, makes city transformation possible. In his book, Dr. Effler explains how a resilient life, characterized by a person's heart and actions, can impact an entire city. In each chapter, Dr. Effler packs practical wisdom gained through the ups and downs of life. My hope is that readers will come to know that their individual inspirational story of resilience can play a certain and pivotal role in enriching the community in which a person lives.

Danny Hesterly
Chattanooga House of Prayer
Danny@chatthop.org

Pastoring provides constant opportunities to walk with people during the worst moments of their lives. Dr. Effler, in "Resilient, Tools For Getting Up After Life Knocks You Down", provides seasoned hard-hitting guidance that is challenging, yet encouraging. This, "all in your business" resource helps both the wounded and the wounded healer move through dark places without allowing pain to take up permanent residence.

Ryan Sharpe
Lead Pastor
Riverhills Church
Tampa, Florida

For
Kristen Towneley Nordgren Effler

The most resilient person I know

Acknowledgements

I heard many years ago, "One is too small a number to achieve anything of significance." Writers know the truth of this statement. The resilient writer knows that 'shared voices' help make the writer's final voice clearer, stronger, and richer.

I am deeply indebted to many people that joined me in this writing sojourn. Without the support, creativity and honesty of the community identified below, this book would not have been possible.

- ⇒ Those I have mentored, guided, and counseled over many years; your vulnerability and willingness to hear truth has always inspired me. Our sessions increased my ability to hear God's voice, and in turn offer needed guidance. Without God's truth and your receptivity to hearing truth, your time would have been wasted and my words, only theory.
- ⇒ A group of leaders, counselors and mental health professionals gathered for Zoom meetings to 'idea share' about the effects of trauma in today's world. These meetings resulted in the birth, development and eventual creation of this book.
- ⇒ Shannon Riese, when I needed a critical mind and sensitive heart to help organize data from a national survey on resiliency and put these findings into a readable format, you were there for me. More than multiple abilities and constant availability, your friendship means much more. If friendship could be measured, I would consider myself one of the wealthiest persons alive.
- ⇒ The 400 survey participants who provided the research data for our national study on resiliency (Chapter Four). These findings and evaluations substantiated the fragile reality that our culture finds itself in today. The numbers do not lie and neither does people's pain.
- ⇒ Our Wednesday night group at *City Church* in Chattanooga jumped into the deep end of this material and became a sounding board and, a 'living lab'. Each week walls became windows; our conversations were heart-shaping and

invaluable. Our times together made it clear this book needed to 'get out there'.

⇒ Dozens of manuscript readers, from California to Wisconsin, Arizona, South Carolina, Florida, and in between, thank you for taking time to read drafts of this manuscript. I needed your input!

⇒ New friends that offered a log cabin to get away, hibernate, and air my brain during a time of personal painful reflection, thank you. (The writing of this manuscript launched me into a deeper dive into my own life, and surfaced questions that I had not previously considered.)

⇒ My own family watched, listened, and read portions of my writing. With their permission, I share their stories; *families pay a certain price for an author's finished work.* I have no words, only great appreciation for their patient and honest support.

⇒ To the editorial, design, and management teams at Penguin publishing who delivered this project…thank you.

Dr. Bill Effler
Apison, Tennessee
February, 2024

CONTENTS

Author's Introduction — I
Other Resources By Bill Effler — IV
Readiness Questionaire — V
Foreword — VII

Part One: Resilience and Why it Matters

Chapter One The Resilient Life — 4
Chapter Two The Need For Resiliency — 18
Chapter Three An Unlikely Community — 34
Chapter Four *You Said It!* — 48

Part Two: Resilience and How it Works

Chapter Five Rewiring Your Brain — 66
Chapter Six Rejecting Your Triggers — 80
Chapter Seven Releasing Your Past — 98
Chapter Eight Reclaiming Your Future — 118

A Final Word: "Suddenly" — 132
Author's Favorite Resilient Realities — 137
Bibliography — 139
Author Description — 143

Author's Introduction

Why a book on resiliency?

Resilient, Tools for Getting Up After Life Knocks You Down started when I was invited to join a group of counselors, social workers, and community leaders via Zoom to share ideas on how people can get their lives back after being "knocked down". During our conversations, the idea of resiliency surfaced again and again. One question during these conversations has stayed with me, "Why is it that our parents, and their parents who went through the Great Depression and their parents (many of which immigrated to the United States before them), seem to have had a resiliency that we do not see in today's culture?" This question deserves an honest answer. Answer: *We do not have the same level of resilience today as in previous generations. Or at least, resilience looks very different.* When no one was looking, the world changed, and no one was prepared for the cultural makeover. Culture will wait in vain for the clock to turn back. Therefore, addressing resiliency with today's cultural complexities is a risky and painful task. Having written and published a counseling book previously[1] and working in higher education at the time, I was invited to write a proposal that would address resiliency in a relevant, practical, and informed way.

My research, reflection, and writing revealed my outdated assumptions that needed to be stripped away. Honest comments from friends, colleagues, and family members revealed my well-protected insecurities. My writing took on a different tone, as I was no longer able to be propped up with cliche-ridden ideas. People reading portions of the manuscript commented the writing often reads like a journal. I confess I have written to myself, as well as you! *Resilient* was written from the context of personal, relational, and professional 'knockdowns.' My own experiences as a pastor, educator, and counselor provided the seedbed from which I could offer proven best practices for 'getting back up' when disappointment occurred. I pray that the principles and stories shared would activate 'something' in the reader's life; such activation will require risk. And if you risk, you will experience what I have, a far more meaningful life.

---

[1] Effler, Bill. *Out From the Shadows, Biblical Counseling Revealed in the Story of Creation.* (Bloomington: Westbow Press, a division of Thomas Nelson books. 2014)

Allow me to tell you who this book is not written for. I am not writing for the person who feels satisfied with their life. Over the years, I have heard people say they are satisfied with their life, marriage, or job, only to discover they had settled for less. I make this statement about the 'satisfied life' because my writing created in me the desire to seek a more resilient way to live. I share one preliminary principle of resiliency that I experienced during my writing: the opportunity to become resilient can come upon a person *quite unexpectedly*. This idea of 'resilience as a surprise' is seen throughout the pages of this book. Setting aside nearly forty years of what I thought resilient living was, I learned resilience *is not* sheer optimism, trying harder, having a brighter marketing idea, or 'having more skills or experience than the next person.' Resiliency is an *interior character quality* that changes the external trajectory and perception of the world that surrounds a person. Yes, success achieves goals and tells a person what they are good at, but resilience is different. Resilient living accomplishes goals, but a resilient life inspires others to rise above things they must overcome.

Especially since COVID, there has been a rejuvenated interest in the topic of resiliency for both professional counselors and those seeking to 'move on' with their lives.[2] Much of what we know today about resilience was not even a thought as I was starting my career. The reader will find that the culmination of my personal and professional experiences has uniquely prepared me to address the topic of resilient living. Through research, a national survey, practical lessons, and personal stories, the reader will discover what the resilient life looks like after overcoming a disappointment. After accepting a painful reality (end of a relationship, a medical diagnosis, any disappointment), the power of determined resilience places a person on the road to healing. The pages of this book offer how to live a resilient life and identify ways to help others discover the gift of resiliency. At the end of every chapter, I have included "resilient realities"; these targeted ideas are designed to stir and focus the reader's mind.

---

[2] Since the outbreak of COVID in 2020, the number of books and articles on resiliency that have been published is astonishing. Most recent research on resilience identifies the importance of mental and emotional regulation, impulse control, self-advocacy, and community. Each of these vital components are addressed and play a vital role in, 'the resilient life'.

The resilient person recognizes and faces a life barrier. The overcomer learns, "The joy of the Lord is my strength."[3] Failure to embark on the journey of resiliency imprisons a person in the past and robs them of promised joy. If anticipated "joy" is one key that unlocks the future, worry paralyzes a person in the present. The reader would be encouraged to hear the words of holocaust survivor Corrie Ten Boom, "God does not have problems, only plans. Worry does not empty tomorrow of its sorrow as much as it robs one of today's strength."

So now we begin together on a journey that may generate thoughts and feelings you did not know existed. If the reader turns just two pages over, a "Readiness Questionnaire" will be found. This short survey will show a person how receptive they might be to experiencing or perhaps starting a resilient life.

Again, welcome!

~ Bill Effler
Apison, Tennessee
February, 2024

---

[3] Nehemiah 8.10

OTHER RESOURCES BY BILL EFFLER

Open Door podcast

Out From the Shadows,
Biblical Counseling
Revealed in the Story of Creation

Mission of the Church,
Practical Theology for
the Twenty First Century

Turning the Church, Inside Out

Those wishing to contact Dr. Effler
for speaking engagements or additional
resources may do so at:

Dr. Bill Effler

weffler@epbfi.com

11936 McGhee Road

Apison, TN. 37302

READINESS QUESTIONNAIRE

There is a reason you picked up this book. An 'inner voice' has probably whispered to you on more than one occasion, "there has got to be more to life than what I am experiencing." People are more than willing to talk about personal growth and satisfaction, but these same people are hesitant to change. Change comes before growth in the dictionary, and in life. Before reading further, take only five minutes to respond to the eight questions below; do not overthink these questions. Your 'inner voice' will tell you how open you are to starting a new life.

Circle the number that corresponds to how much you agree or disagree with each statement.

1 - Strongly disagree (SD)
2 - Disagree (D)
3 - Agee (A)
4 - Strongly agree (SA)

	SD 1	D 2	A 3	SA 4
1. I am fairly happy with most areas in my current life.	1	2	3	4
2. I do not easily welcome new ideas.	1	2	3	4
3. I think I may need to make some changes in my life.	1	2	3	4
4. I hope this material helps me to better understand myself.	1	2	3	4
5. I have taken steps to remove obstacles in my life.	1	2	3	4
6. I have made important changes in my life, but more are needed.	1	2	3	4
7. I get concerned that I might slip back into old habits.	1	2	3	4
8. I still struggle from time to time with basic discipline.	1	2	3	4

Direction: Add up the numbers for items 1 & 2; 3 & 4, 5 & 6, 7 & 8.

You will see which category below you scored the highest.

~ Responses to items 1 & 2 = "before change" score: _____
~ Responses to items 3 & 4 = "thinking about change" score: _____
~ Responses to items 5 & 6 = "action" score: _____
~ Responses to items 7 & 8 = "maintenance" score: _____

INTERPRETATION.

The *highest score* in the "before change" category indicates a person most likely does not see the need to change much of anything in their life. Perhaps some of the ideas presented in this book might challenge existing ways a person views their life. If the *highest score* was in the "thinking about change" category, a person has thought that there may be a need to make some life changes, but no significant action has been taken. If the *highest number* is in the "action" category a person has probably made some changes in their life but recognizes more changes are still needed. If the *highest score* was in the "maintenance" category a person has seen significant change or improvement in their life that they are proud of but sustaining personal growth is a concern. *Regardless the category of where a person sees themselves, the ideas presented in this book will help in living a more successful and meaningful life.*

Foreword

"The world is hungry for the truth and practicality found in
Resilient!"
Dr. Vikki Waters

I wish someone had given me this book years ago. While reading, I discovered unexplored and yet-to-be-healed places in my own heart. Over the years, people have said to me, "I should be able to quickly recover from something that sidelines me for a season or even seasons." Or, perhaps you've heard it said, "suck it up, buttercup," and think this belief is what some call perseverance. Here's the truth in this book: *Resilience* is *not the same* as perseverance or "sucking it up" after being knocked down. Resilience is a God-given gift. God will help you because your story matters to God. Your journey is significant to Him. God wants to help you learn how to recover from life's knockdowns. Know that God is presently involved in your life in every way.

Resilient is a powerful heart-healing tool in your toolbelt! Suppose you are ready to say "No" to dwelling on your problems, playing the victim, living in a state of hypervigilance, unhealthy coping mechanisms, or being weighed down with depression and anxiety. In that case, this book will be of tremendous help. You will not only get up and become stronger but become able to withstand difficulty and experience freedom, hope, and purpose. As you dive into this transformative message, you will be deeply touched by Bill's own story, humor, creative writing, practicality, and transparency. You will find for yourself a trusted friend who will lead you to the True source of resilience. You will be drawn to the tangible presence of Father God, Jesus, and the Holy Spirit, who are for you, with you, and in you.

I can tell you Bill and his wife, Kris, are the real deal. He is a trusted and genuine brother in Christ and will be the same for you. He carries a powerful anointing on his life; he is a truth-teller who causes a person to stop and lean deeply into Jesus. Most of all, he has unmistakable ways of inviting the inbreaking presence of God into a person's deepest pain. As a valued friend and colleague, I am excited to recommend *Resilient* to you. With expectation, I know readers will lay hold of and begin a resilient life.

Dr. Vikki Waters, D.Min

Founder, Growing in Grace Ministries, Chattanooga, TN.
Heart Healing Coach,
Bestselling Author, *Lasting Freedom: Taking Back Your Authority in Christ for Every Area of Your Life,* and *Loved Like Jesus*

Part One | Resilience and Why it Matters

Part One: Resilience and Why it Matters

Chapter One: The Resilient Life: Understanding the Need for More

Chapter Two: The Need for Resiliency: Understanding Pain and Suffering

Chapter Three: An Unlikely Community: Understanding the Need for Others

Chapter Four: "You Said It!": Resiliency instrument and national field results of inventories

CHAPTER ONE

The Resilient Life

> The world breaks everyone; afterward, many are stronger in the broken places.
> — Ernest Hemingway

> Though he may stumble, he will not fall, for the LORD upholds him with his hand.
> — Psalm 37.24 (NIV)

> When we can no longer change a situation, we must learn to change ourselves.
> — Viktor Frankl

Chapter Summary

- Introducing resiliency
- Author's experiences with resiliency
- Why people avoid resiliency
- Myths and benefits of resiliency

Introducing resiliency

Have you ever thought, "I wish I could just start over?" You looked at your finances and wondered, "How did I get so much debt?" Perhaps you made a hasty decision and later thought, "If I only knew then what I know now..." Many "if only I..." statements describe the desire to start any number of things over. At times, a person's life can resemble a slowly running computer. When a computer noticeably slows down, technicians perform what is referred to as a "reboot" (a 'shut down and start over' is attempted to regain original factory efficiency).[4] The first step needed to reboot life like a slowly running computer *is to*

---

[4] God's original Kingdom design found in Genesis 1.28f. for living was threefold; be fruitful, multiply and bring order to all of creation. This 'stool' of three legs can be understood to mean, to achieve *initial* success, multiple any success that has been accomplished and, be responsible to bring order to all that which God has placed before a person.

acknowledge reality. Acknowledging reality is the most important *initial step needed* to achieve personal transformation. The second step to the rebooted life is found in the word resiliency. The resilient person chooses to *move through whatever challenge is before them with identified purpose and intentionality.*[5] Again, the first step to 'getting on with life' after a disappointment occurs is to acknowledge reality. A second step is to predetermine to 'move forward,' which I refer to as the practice of resilience.

Starting over is part of the economy of God. Scripture includes multiple stories of God offering an invitation to begin life again. Jacob was a deceiver. Samson was a womanizer. Jonah was a run-away prophet. A classic case study of an individual offered a 'start over' is Peter, a man whose life is consumed with veneered spiritual superiority. Peter, like those mentioned previously, failed miserably. The proverb, "pride goes before a fall, "underlies most people's poor decisions."[6] Each of the above examples shows that God offers second chances; God promises to exchange "beauty where there were once only ashes."[7] The God of scripture is the God of the comeback. A person's biggest setback or mistake could be a stepping stone to an amazing future! I SO believe this and want you to consider believing this, too.

I am attracted to the future-oriented thinking of God, as spoken through his messenger Isaiah, "See, I am doing a new thing! Now it springs up; do you not perceive it? I am making a way in the wilderness and streams in the wasteland."[8] The reference to a *'new thing'* implies that the past *is past.* This 'new thing' is *recognizable, springs up* seemingly *out of nowhere,* and there will be a sure and certain *"way"* that leads a person out of their wilderness-like life. This new direction provides "streams in the desert" that quenches the thirst of a dry-mouthed person who perhaps had once thought, "That drink may be offered to others, but certainly not to me." A resilient life is marked by freedom, hope, and purpose. A resilient life is profoundly

---

[5] 'Resiliency' does not imply a lack of stress, only the ability to live with stress and overcome its challenges.
[6] Proverbs 16.18
[7] Isaiah 61. 3
[8] Isaiah 43.19.

'present-future' focused. The forward-looking words of the apostle Paul were an invitation to the audience he addressed in his day when he said, "...one thing I do: *forgetting what is behind* and I strain *toward* what is *ahead*."[9] This same invitation is ours too.

As stated previously, the practice of resilience begins by acknowledging reality and intentionally taking steps to move through adversity. Hank Aaron, hall of fame baseball player and one-time home run king, said his life motto was, "Keep swinging." Aaron's "keep swinging" motto typifies resiliency. Resiliency can apply to everyone, from housewives to business executives, students, landscapers, or a person just coming out of jail. If a person can harness the power that resiliency unleashes, there is no limit to what a person can accomplish. The ability to acknowledge reality and begin life again empowers a person to 'keep swinging.' Resiliency is helpful in the workplace (i.e., navigating a job change, downsizing, expansion, termination, even a promotion), education (to complete coursework and graduate), sport (the process of rehabilitation that leads to restored skill), and marriage. Certainly, one can also include emotional resiliency (the ability to harness one's emotions and feelings) as well as mental resiliency (an ability to regulate or control one's thinking so thoughts can be healthfully expressed). Resiliency is the 'secret sauce' that empowers a successful life. I do not want to be misunderstood here; there is no 'secret' to living resiliently, only seeking hard after Christ and personal determination.

Again, there is absolutely no end to where resiliency or getting a second chance cannot be applied. This first chapter introduces key components and themes that relate to the resilient life. As we begin, I offer a critical idea that cannot be overlooked: if a life challenge or setback is ignored, justified, or grossly minimized, one forfeits the possibility of having a resilient life. In reading this last observation, a dear counselor friend and mentor to me stated, "If one does not see how Christ makes a difference within the issues of life, this person would have missed the full potential of a resilient life."[10]

---

[9] Philippians 3.8 , New International Version
[10] I need to say here as I begin, no book is ever written alone. I am so very thankful for people like Kirk Lewis, who has written extensively on what he calls

My experiences with resiliency

The need for resiliency and the successful practice of it has played a significant role in my life. Following both undergraduate and graduate school studies, I spent the first 18 years of my professional career as a pastor in California, serving in a variety of positions, including that of Senior Pastor. I also worked as an intake counselor at a residential treatment facility in these early years. After moving to Southeastern Tennessee, I joined the *Lee University* faculty, where I would teach and mentor undergraduate students for the next 22 years of my career. During this same time, I also became a board member of the Southeastern chapter of the *Alzheimer's Association*, a published author, counselor in private practice, and consulted with both churches and the business world. In *every* professional and personal arena, refining would await me personally and professionally. Today, I recognize Spirit-based resiliency (an adding or enhancing to) as an indispensable quality needed in professional and personal development.[11] For a person to not recognize their limitations creates a liability for them and potentially harms those with whom they work. Stated differently, a person with no accountability in their life becomes a liability to everyone around them. Dan Reiland has written, "God never intended our weakness to become permission for excuses but rather, reminders to us that He is the source of our strength."[12]

Being very transparent, the need for resilient living has not been limited to my professional life. Nine years ago, our son was diagnosed with cancer. Time stopped for our family; time seems to stand still during a challenging season of life. Fast forward to New Year's Eve morning five months later, my wife awoke in this same calendar year,

---

"Desperate Dependency". Kirk might say, to live resiliently is to live with "desperate dependency" on Christ.

[11] A person's character will include both *hard* skills (tasks, functions and areas that may require specific training) and *soft* skills (communication, personal attributes, social awareness). When I have spoken with those in the 'hiring loop' I have been told, repeatedly, that hard skills are what a person is hired for, but soft skills are what gives a person professional longevity. Further, one HR person told me, 'It is difficult to teach soft skills. If they are not recognizable in the interview, the interview ends.'

[12] Dan Reiland, *The Pastor's Coach*, "How Leadership Weakness Becomes Strength With God", April 16, 2023

saying, "I am blind." I have detailed both my wife's and son's stories in my former book, *Out From the Shadows, Biblical Counseling Revealed in the Story of Creation.*[13] It was during both our son's extensive cancer treatments and a series of interventions and surgeries to recapture my wife's eyesight that my wife, Kristen, commented, "Our family is living out the title of your counseling book." No truer words could have captured our family's existence in those chaotic, shadow-laden days. The idea of resilient living is best understood as a season and not as an event. A person may find themselves asking, "Will life ever return to normal?" When anyone finds themself in a transitioning season of any kind, it is common to have a 'hurry up and heal' orientation to life. It would be nice if 'hurry' could be *the rule* in the healing process, but most often, hurry is *the exception* to the rule of healing. Caroline Leaf is right in saying, "When deep hidden wounds are exposed, there is always pain before the healing…"[14] If one believes that "love is patient,"[15] then one must also believe that God's loving and healing presence can be found in the pain as one waits for healing and restoration.

During a painful transitional season in my own life, I practiced unhealthy expressions of coping. These short-cited behaviors had taken up residence like an unwanted house guest that overstays their welcome. I will say more about this in a later chapter, but for now, I will say that the 'uninvited guests' of faulty thinking, late night 'junking out', non-existent exercise, and obsessing over past disappointments 'visited me' regularly. Isolating from possible sources of help was a way for me to hide personal insecurities. Only by addressing unhealthy ways of living and seeking accountability from others was I able to begin to get my life back on track. Rigorous honesty made me a better husband, father, and counselor…a more authentic person. I use the phrase "internal self-work" to describe the transformative process that was released in my life. Yes, "self-work" or self-advocacy is critical to personal transformation. Without

---

[13] Bill Effler, *Out From the Shadows, Biblical Counseling Revealed in the Story of Creation.* Bloomington: Westbow Press, 2014
[14] Caroline Leaf, *Cleaning Up Your Mental Mess.* Grand Rapids: Baker Books, 2023. Pg.83
[15] 1 Corinthians 13.4

hesitation, the most significant changes I needed to make in my life came from God placing other voices into my life so that I could heal. In the early days of 'on again/off again resiliency,' I was taught that the deepest healing a person will receive is never done alone.[16] In the closing days of his life, John the Baptist said to his followers, referring to Jesus, "...this is the time for him to increase and for me to decrease."[17] This statement exemplifies the quality of humility. In referring to his own crucifixion and eventual death, Jesus said, "When the son of man is high and lifted up, he draws all people to himself."[18] *Lasting resiliency often includes humility and a dying to oneself.*

Avoiding Resiliency

Failure to recognize the dysfunctional reality in one's life keeps a person from experiencing resiliency. In his book *Healing is a Choice*, Stephen Arterburn identifies at least three 'pushback' statements[19] a person uses to avoid healthy living. People will say, "It (a painful or frustrating situation) happened such a long time ago." This is a *historical* excuse that prevents a person from getting needed help. People also say, "I'm fine." These words are often a smokescreen that can be understood to mean **f**eelings **i**nside, **n**ot **e**xpressed (and it's none of your......business!). This is a *false emotional* excuse that avoids facing reality. A third pushback remark is, "All I need is God." Arterburn says this statement is a form of denial, and eventually, reality will come seeping out (when the person least expects it). This third pushback statement is a *religious*[20] excuse and is often found in church culture. I add a fourth smokescreen statement, "It's what my parents did, and it worked for them." This is a convenient *family-*

---

[16] Chapter three is dedicated to the vital role that community plays in the resilient life.
[17] John 3.30
[18] John 12.32
[19] "Pushback" is a word to describe a spoken or unspoken message or behavior that people use to essentially communicate to a helper, "I am not ready to go, where you would like to take me". These "pushbacks" are actually boundary statements made by a person in need and must be honored by those in the role of helping.
[20] I do not use the word, "religious", in a positive way. I see "religious people" as shallow and pretentious. One reason why I am comfortable counseling with persons struggling with addictions is because I see a desperation in them, that I do not see with religious people. And I would remind the reader, it was religious people who crucified Jesus.

based excuse.[21] Each of these excuses is like a person smelling smoke (acknowledging potential danger) yet unwilling to discover where the dangerous fire is located. Again, Arterburn's wisdom is helpful for us, "Surrendering to God and allowing God to take over is never easy, but it allows God's infinite healing power to provide the path to healing, rather than our finite and futile attempts at control and manipulation."[22]

Rich Buhler's classic work, *Pain and Pretending,*[23] explains a different way of understanding why people avoid change in their lives. Concerning pain, Buhler identifies constructive pain as something that is both *needed and necessary* in order to accomplish a desired goal. An athlete's off-season workout discipline is often agonizing but results in meeting the goals of increased strength, mobility, and dexterity. This type of pain transforms and empowers the athlete to compete at a higher level of competence and achievement. S*econd,* destructive pain serves no purpose and inflicts senseless harm (by a person or, perhaps, a toxic workplace[24]). When this second type of pain reaches a breaking point, a person's life can be dismantled to the core.[25] Unlike constructive pain and its *transforming* components, destructive pain has no other goal other than to "steal, kill, and destroy." Concerning pretending (ignoring, minimizing, or denying[26]), Buhler says pretending is a form of shock. For example,

---

[21] A close look into a person's family often reveals reasons as to why a person does, what they do. For years I have taught my counseling students that a careful investigating into a person's birth family or, "family of origin" will uncover an entire system that answers the question, "What has caused this person's sense of reality?" Answer, the scripts found in a person's birth family.

[22] Ibid, pg. 17

[23] Rich Buhler, *Pain and Pretending,* (Nashville: Thomas Nelson books, 1991, revised in 1998)

[24] I have consulted with both churches and in the general marketplace only to see rampant and out of control 'toxic leadership'. The reader can be helped by: Gary Chapman's book, *Rising Above a Toxic Workplace* (Chicago: Northfield publishing, 2014) and Ronald Enroth's book, *Churches That Abuse* (Grand Rapids: Zondervan publishing, 1992)

[25] Rich Buhler, *Pain and Pretending,* (Nashville: Thomas Nelson books, 1991, revised in 1998). Pg. 36

[26] To repress pain is an unconscious acknowledgement of pain. A example would be a person having a compound fracture in their leg, a bone is sticking through the skin. The badly wounded person says, "just bring a band aid". Again, repression, is a dishonest stuffing or acknowledgement of, a presenting painful reality.

if you received news right now that a member of your family was killed in an automobile accident, your brain would probably go into shock. That's your mind's way of saying, 'I can't handle this all at once, so I am going to shut down my systems and gently travel into another world for a while so I can survive.'[27]

To ignore, minimize, or deny pain is short-cited. Seasoned counselors are quick to observe that the earlier in life a traumatic or harmful experience occurs (say, in childhood), the greater the likelihood that this same experience becomes a lens through which a person views all of life. Buhler summarizes 'pretending' by saying, "If our childhood pain has been overpowering and we have not learned how to respond to it, we are more likely to be paralyzed by it."[28] This depth of pain ultimately thrusts a person into "another world" (like the automobile story above). I summarize Buhler's contributions on pain and pretending in the following way:

Unprocessed pain, maintained by pretending, creates a false foundation upon which a person builds their life. Pretending creates a false reality. The false reality prevents a person from moving healthfully forward in life. I might even say false reality is possibly a more difficult problem to address than the original or precipitating painful experience.

Avoiding needed change is dangerous. There is no magical way of erasing pain or the adjoining memories that come with a painful experience. I purposely include *memories* of the *actual painful event* because the brain records and stores painful events.[29] An entire chapter later addresses the brain's function and recorded memories. The brain plays a central role in the resilient life. Only by embracing pain can a person experience the life that God intends for every person. Failure to embrace pain will not result in freedom. On the very night of his betrayal from a trusted friend, Jesus went "a little further" to pray, saying, "If there is any other way..."[30] Jesus' prayer and

---

[27] Ibid, pg. 151
[28] Ibid, pg. 36
[29] Bessel Van Der Kolk, *The Body Keeps the Score: Brain, Mind and Body in the Healing of Trauma* (New York: Penguin Books, 2014)
[30] Matthew 26.39

ultimate submission to his father's will demonstrate a willingness to be led where others will not go.[31] Many reboots require a person to "go further." Going further results in making healthier choices that result in an empowered life. Once a person realizes there is a need to go further with God and face pain, a person will discover the events that once brought devastation now transform life in unimagined ways.

During my writing, I was reminded of a particular portion of the poem, *A Road Not Taken* by Robert Frost,

> Two roads diverged in a yellow wood, and sorry
> I could not travel both. And be one traveler,
> long I stood and looked down as far as I could to
> where it bent in the undergrowth....
> Two roads diverged in a wood, and I—
> *I took the one less traveled by,*
> *And that has made all the difference.*[32]

Jesus' 'road taken' would lead to crucifixion and death. Upon the cross, Jesus prayed, "Father, forgive them, for they know not what they do."[33] Resilient living often includes some expression of *forgiveness*. While caught in the clutches of the cross, Jesus showed his ultimate humanity as he cried out, "My God, my God, why have you forsaken me ..."[34] During a vicious and cruel life experience, a person's mind can be flooded with feelings of *total abandonment*. Jesus' question from the cross, "Why?" demonstrates total transparency and is an ultimate example of Jesus' humanity. If Jesus cried out with such a visceral lament, should not his followers also be allowed to do the same?[35] Jesus' final prayer exemplifies his complete ability to embrace extreme adversity, "Into your hands, I commit my spirit...."[36] Perhaps the clearest example of a resilient life, as modeled by Jesus, is a life fully submitted to God, *especially when* life does not

---

[31] Henri Nouwen, *In the Name of Jesus*, (New York: Crossroad Books, 1999) Pg. 62
[32] Robert Frost, *A Road Not Taken*. I have cited only a portion of this work. A complete rendition can be found on line. I have added my own italics, for emphasis.
[33] Luke 23.34
[34] Matthew 27.46 and Mark 15.34
[35] Philip Yancy has built a writing carrier on the subject of, 'the silence of God'. Any of his several books are well worth investigating.
[36] Luke 23.46

go as planned. In like manner, resilient living should mirror the life of Jesus.

Myths and benefits of resilience

Myths surrounding resilience

The first myth concerning change and resilience is that *facts make people change.* False. Whether a person is consumed with a life-altering substance (including prescription medication) or a successful businessperson addicted to themselves, people who are *not* reality-based *never* respond to facts, *ever.* Fact-finding, rule-keeping, and endless analysis *without relational investment* will result in a blowup *every time.*

A second myth is that the quest to live resiliently (or enjoy a sustained change) takes a long time. False. If Covid has taught us anything, it is that change can happen *quickly.* A third myth concerning resiliency is that *threatening a person is an effective catalyst for change.* False. Research in individual and corporate change reveals that instilling fear or making a threat of any kind is counterproductive; if any change is seen, the change is not sustainable[37]. A fourth myth concerning a life adjustment is that *change can be avoided.* False. Of the four myths mentioned, this one is the most ludicrous. One needs only apply this myth to the human body or aging. Anyone's body tells them they are 'changing.' A bathroom scale and the 'mirror on the wall' tell the truth about changes that are happening before our eyes.

Some readers may think at this early point, "The idea of resiliency sounds overwhelming." Before I identify the benefits of resilient living, I offer the following idea to consider: without change, there can be no breakthrough, and without a breakthrough, life will remain 'same 'ol, same 'ol'. To seriously consider either personal or corporate change, one must face reality. Allow me a cinema reference to address the significance of facing reality. I admit to being a fan of the *Rocky* film series starring Sylvester Stallone. In the *Rocky III* film, Rocky has now become the undisputed champion of the boxing world. A new and hungry contender, 'Clubber Lang' (played by Mr. T), appears on

---

[37] *Forbes* magazine, routinely, publishes articles on this reality.

the scene and wants a shot at the title. "Mick" (played by Burgess Meredith), Rocky's faithful and trusted manager, growls, "You can't beat him, kid, he will kill ya within the first three rounds!" Rocky objects. Then, Mick shares the hard and necessary truth about Rocky's *unrecognized* reality. Mick says, "What has happened to you happens to most great fighters. Y*ou've become civilized.*" Only Christ can offer people the character quality of resilience that leads to resilient living, as compared to "civilized living". "Civilized living" is not reality-based and has behaviors and/or beliefs that do not promote healthy living. The civilized person surrounds themselves with other unhealthy people who help maintain the mascarade of resiliency. In short, "civilized people" settle for less than what Christ can offer.

The 'civilized life' lacks grit, confidence, and perseverance. In the words of Jesus, a person has "life," but not to the full.[38] Resiliency results in a person's ability to "fight the good fight."[39] The "good fight" that Paul describes to his young protégé, Timothy, takes courage. God knows that life on earth is a fight and that our frail, sinful inclination is to cave into fear or, worse yet, disobey God's design for our lives. <u>Consider this:</u> God knows our fearfulness and lack of capability, BUT God still calls us "friends."[40] Just as Paul encouraged Timothy in his fight, each of us needs a 'Paul' to encourage us in challenging times. Moses needed to encourage his wilderness-wandering people by saying, "Do not be afraid. Stand firm, and you will see the deliverance that the Lord will bring today. The Egyptians you see today you will never see again. The Lord will fight for you; you need only to be still."[41] When facing even a small change, the strongest of persons need a Paul or Moses to be a source of encouragement as one foot is placed in front of the other.

Benefits of resiliency

There is a near-endless list of benefits to living a resilient life, but I offer only four as I close. First, the resilient person *learns something new about themselves*. Because a challenge has been faced and

---

[38] John 10.10
[39] 2 Timothy 4.7
[40] John 15.15
[41] Exodus 14. 13,14

overcome, a person may say, "I didn't know I could do this!" Second, a resilient *person lives life with less anxiety*. Extremely undisciplined people suffer from a tremendous load of anxiety. These people carry with them a host of "could of" and "should of" statements. If a mentor or counselor can help identify one step in achieving a goal, anxiety can be reduced.[42] A third benefit of resilient living is *a boost in a person's self-esteem*. Reason tells us that success over anything reduces stress and brings with it increased confidence! A fourth benefit of resilient living is that the person *meets new friends, helpers, and voices of encouragement*. In short, this person learns that life was never intended to be lived alone.

As I was writing this chapter, I realized many of the new directions in my current new stage of life came from unlikely sources. Upon first hearing, suggestions made to me by others were often unwelcome voices. Yet, the voices of others were only seeking to introduce God's better way, a 'road less traveled.' In writing this manuscript, I sent drafts of my writing to many different types of people from all walks of life. These outside voices saw things that I did not see. Even now, I am reminded of Isaiah's prophecy, "…Seek the Lord while he may be found; call on him while he is near...For my thoughts are not your thoughts, neither are your ways my ways. As the heavens are higher than the earth, *so are my ways higher than your ways*…"[43] God's ways are always beneficial for those who chase after Him.

Resilient realities …

- o Acknowledging reality may very well be the most important step needed to achieve personal transformation.
- o A 'reboot' is a first step towards one's future, whereas 'resiliency' is a process of many steps that leads to personal freedom.
- o If a life challenge or setback is ignored, justified, or grossly minimized, one forfeits the possibility of a resilient life.

---

[42] Charles Allen Koller in *Solution Focused Pastoral Counseling* refers to this strategy as "co-creating goals" with the seeker.
[43] Isaiah 55. 6, 8

- For a person to not recognize their limitations creates a liability for them and can also bring even greater harm to those with whom they work.
- A lasting reboot often includes humility and a dying to oneself.
- Once a person realizes the need to go further with God and face their pain, they will discover that the events that once brought devastation now transform life in unimagined ways.
- Without change, there can be no breakthrough; without breakthroughs or reboots, there can be no future.
- Upon first hearing, many suggestions from others are unwelcome voices. Yet, I would learn my friends and mentors were only seeking to introduce me to God's better way, a 'road less traveled.'

CHAPTER TWO

The Need for Resiliency

"All battles are first won or lost, in the mind."
Joan of Arc

The battles we fight are not of flesh and blood,
but our help does not come from flesh and blood, either.

Chapter Summary

- ➤ The reality of spiritual warfare
- ➤ The journey through suffering
- ➤ The victim mindset
- ➤ A believer's mental health
- ➤ The benefits of unexplainable loss
- ➤ Jesus and the pain of separation
- ➤ The path forward: Paul's thorn in the flesh, explained

The reality of spiritual warfare

The Christian life is a battle. Spiritual warfare is real.[44] Angels are real.[45] Demons are real.[46]

The apostle John tells us the whole world lies under the power of the evil one.[47] Scripture instructs, "Resist the devil."[48] Satan is described

---

[44] Multiple places in scripture speak of a war in the 'spirit realm'. I emphasize here a believer's assured victory over the spirit realm of darkness as described in Psalm 121. 3,7&8; Colossians 2.15; Philippians 1.5; Ephesian 6.1f.

[45] Judith McNutt. *Angels Are For Real.* (Bloomington: Chosen Books. 2012). The subject of angels is really a 'lost' subject amongst many believers. However, in this introductory work, Judith McNutt offers a very readable introduction to a very necessary subject.

[46] The Bible tells us that demons are fallen angels who joined Satan in his rebellion against God and who were defeated and cast out of heaven along with Satan (Revelation 12:7-9).

[47] 1 John 5.19
[48] James 4.4

in 1 Peter 5.8 as a "roaring lion, seeking anyone to devour," and in the verse following, readers are commanded to oppose this intimidating presence and stand firm in faith. In the Old Testament book of Job, Satan is portrayed as a determined presence, "... roaming throughout the earth, going back and forth on it."[49] A few verses later, we read God grants Satan limited access to Job's life.[50] As in Job's time, today, demons have influence and a degree of liberty, but the influence of the evil one is limited.[51] Eventually, all expressions of evil will be destroyed, and evil's defeat will be complete. Disobedient living relegates a person to a place of total separation from God and any sense of hope.

Dutch Sheets comments on the activities of the evil one by saying,

> "The serpent was craftier than any beast. The Hebrew word for "crafty" carries with it the concept of being bare or smooth. We still use the concept of crafty today when we speak of someone as being cunning in a bad sense, saying to them that they are slick or perhaps a smooth operator.... [Satan] is far more effective with his slick craftiness than with his power or strength."[52]

The muttering lies of the enemy must be recognized and silenced.[53] *Especially during times of despair*, a believer's mind must readily declare, "If God is for us, who can be against us?"[54] *This robust*

---

[49] Job 1.17
[50] Job 1.12
[51] Job 1.12 records that the Lord said to Satan, "...everything he has is under your power, but on the man himself do not lay a finger." This text indicates that Satan has power and influence, but it is a limited influence.
[52] Dutch Sheets is quoted in Chuck Pierce's book, *Prayers that Outwit the Enemy*. (Ventura: Regal books, 2004)
   pgs. 7,8
[53] In John 8.44 Jesus refers to Satan as the "father of lies"; lying is Satan's native language just as "truth" (Jn. 14.6) is Jesus' natural and spiritual language.
[54] Romans 8.31

declaration of faith is an 'in your face' attitude against the enemy and a supreme act of spiritual warfare. A spiritual conflict of any kind demands gutsy willpower that is nothing short of determination fueled by God-given strength. This depth of determination unleashes untapped resiliency. The intent of this chapter is not to elevate the significance of evil but rather to bring to the reader's attention a greater awareness of evil's influence.[55] In the following pages, the reader will be encouraged with biblical and practical truths that are essential when facing a gathering storm of unexplainable hardship.

The journey *through* suffering

I do not believe all tragedy comes from evil, but certainly, some do. However, when unthinkable suffering occurs, resilient living is mandatory. A part of resiliency is having an ongoing intentional mindset that is determined to get back up after life knocks a person down. Now, after forty years of combined full-time work as a pastor, educator, and counselor, I know my mind is a commonplace the enemy attacks. I personally know that when the enemy stirs distraction or confusion into my life, my thinking, behavior, and emotions are at risk. Bessel Van Der Kolk comments in his book, *The Body Keeps the Score*, "The greatest source of personal pain are the lies we believe *about ourselves.*"[56] Mental discipline and faith-filled living must be grounded in the word of God. A life committed to reading and reflecting on the word of God regularly is one way of understanding what it means to "walk in the Spirit."[57]

When a 'missel of injustice' has been fired into one's life, thoughts are easily highjacked. Researchers of the brain tell us the brain recognizes and records both life-threatening and life-giving experiences. When either of these occurs, the brain *instinctively releases* chemicals. Once the brain is chemically fueled and exhilarated, slowing down a

---

[55] A more recently published book on the unseen reality of the spiritual realm is Dawna De Silva's book, *Shifting Atmosphere, Discerning and Displacing the Spiritual Forces Around You* (Shippensburg: Destiny Image books. 2017)
[56] Bessel Van Der Kolk, *The Body Keeps The Score*, (New York: Penguin Books, 2014). Italics added for emphasis
[57] Galatians 5.16

person's thoughts or actions is near impossible.[58] For nearly four decades, I have tried to help people work through losses that were no fault of their own. Often, the challenges of others challenged my own mental and emotional strength. As a young pastor and new father, I still recall now, decades later, my first infant graveside service; I had more tears than words.[59] In agonizing times like this, one's foundational beliefs about God and oneself can be shaken to the core.

Whether one is faced with a 'minor upset' or a 'major loss,' the biblical text of James 1. 2-4 offers one initial starting point for the individual who seeks to move through a season of unrest. James writes ....

> "My brothers, count (or consider) it all joy when you fall into various trials, knowing that the testing of your faith produces patience. But let patience have its perfect work, that you may be perfect and complete, lacking nothing.[60]

This portion of scripture explains that suffering tests a person's faith and that God's testing is purposeful and productive, yields patience, and, in the end, demonstrates the perfect will of God.[61] James' words, "count or consider," direct the reader to *begin* the journey of suffering by *engaging the mind*. Yet, when faced by a trial of any kind, a person's natural tendency is to NOT engage the mind. When thinking is the last action taken during heartache, heartbreak is not far behind.

James says that when the journey of suffering and pain has run its course, a person will "lack nothing." What does James mean that a person will "lack nothing"? What about when tragedy takes

---

[58] I will devote an entire chapter on the significance of our brain's chemistry and how the brain can either empower resiliency and stability or catastrophically derail the forward movement of life.

[59] Most ministerial training does not include teaching or guidance on helping people walk through the death of an infant. These early professional experiences can carry with them a certain element of PTSD in the life of a young pastor. These professional memories can linger for many years, as is the case with me.

[60] James 1. 2-4, NKJV

[61] It was not my intent to identify these four "Ps" yet, they are still worthy of reflection and discussion.

something of great value? How does anyone live through great loss and *not believe* that something of significance has *not been* lost? Have you ever lost a baby before it was born? My wife and I have. Have you ever been professionally betrayed? I have. Have you been with people who said they cared for you, but you feel *emotionally abandoned?* I have. <u>Hard reality</u>: There are certain losses that a person will experience where life will never again return to its former state. Unanswered questions will remain. The difficult choice to move on with life will be a necessary, difficult, and determined decision. I am sure some readers know of this difficult life reality. R. T. Kendall is one of my favorite authors in the field of mental health and spiritual direction. In facing the deep pain that I have been addressing, Kendall writes, "You are probably at your sanest when you come to the place where you abandon all except your desire for God."[62]

Before moving on to a believer's mental health, I want to showcase what might be the most common byproduct that surfaces when a person believes they have been attacked and or have been unfairly treated. What I am referring to is what has been called a 'victim mentality.' Many signs indicate a victim mentality is at work. Below are only a few:

- o A well-practiced script of how and why life is miserable.
- o Unregulated or uncontrolled emotional reactions.
- o The overwhelming need to have pain validated by others.
- o The belief is that they always get the 'short end of the stick' as compared to others.
- o Insecurity drives a person to surround themselves with people they know will not challenge them.
- o The belief that a painful experience or circumstance is unique to them.
- o An inability to break agreement with the pain of the past.
- o There is an increasing *inability* to hear from God.

A hard truth about trying to help a person with a victim mentality is that some people prefer and choose victimization over liberation.

---

[62] R. T. Kendall, *The Parables of Jesus: A Guide to Understanding and Applying the Stories Jesus Told* (Grand Rapids: Baker Books, 2008), pg. 53

This is clearly seen in John 5 when Jesus asks the crippled man at the pool, "Do you want to get well?"[63] Like a good friend, a person's victim script is all they know. Taking their script from them would force a person to address the excuses and their role in maintaining their victim mindset.

A believer's mental health

I want to speak specifically to *suffering and the mental health of the believer*. The process of recovering one's life while caught in the clutches of loss is not clean or straightforward. The development of the *believer's emotional and mental health state carries* a unique back-and-forth element. One example of this back-and-forth living, seen in the life of a believer, is when a person prays only to take back the surrendered concern into one's own hands. Paul was aware of his own spiritual inconsistencies as he wrote to the believers in Rome ~

> *I'm a mystery to myself.* 16 I want to do what is right but end up doing what my moral instincts condemn…my behavior is not in line with my desire…. I am a human being made of flesh and trafficked as a slave. 17 And now I realize that it is no longer my true self doing it, but the unwelcome intruder of sin in my humanity. 18 For I know that nothing good lives within the flesh of my fallen humanity. The longings to do what is right are within me, but willpower is not enough to accomplish it. 19 My lofty desires to do what is good are dashed when I do the very things I want to avoid…. 22 *Truly, deep within my true identity, I love to do what pleases, but I discern another power operating in my humanity, waging war against the moral that that sabotages me…* 24 this unwelcome intruder in my humanity. What an agonizing situation I am in![64]

When considering losses that alter a person's mental health, Stormie Omaritan offers her own vantage point concerning

---

[63] John 5.6
[64] Romans 7. 15-24, *The Message* translation. Italics included for author's emphasis.

optimal emotional and spiritual health, "... emotional health is having total peace about who you are, what you're doing, and where you're going...it's feeling totally at peace about the past, present, and future. It's knowing you are in line with God's ultimate purpose for you and being fulfilled in that."[65]

The emotional health described by Omaritan is available and achievable. *However*, the quality of life that Omaritan describes most often comes *after* the storm has passed. During times of excruciating loss, people experience a lack of peace; purpose is questioned, and understanding the future is sheer guesswork. Overcoming emotional and mental turmoil is a process that does not come in a day, from a book, podcast, counseling session, or single bible passage.[66]

Following the death of his wife Joy, after only three years of marriage, C.S. Lewis wrote, "Her absence is like the sky, spread over everything."[67] And later would write, "God whispers to us in our pleasures, speaks to us in our conscience, but shouts to us in our pain; it is his megaphone to rouse a deaf world."[68] I say again, after the gathering storm has passed, a person better understands, *in part,* the purpose or reason of their painful season. During a 'season of uncertainty,' the ability to hear God is a common challenge. Lysa TerKeurst offers her understanding of how our culture commonly faces pain, "Feeling the pain is the first step toward healing the pain. The longer we avoid the feeling, the more we delay our healing. We can numb it, ignore it, or pretend it doesn't exist, but all those options lead to an eventual breakdown, not a breakthrough."[69] A scriptural example of a person who was deeply in line with God's ultimate purpose for his life despite his ominous hardship was the Old

---

[65] Stormie Omaritan, *Lord, I Want To Be Whole*, (Nashville: Thomas Nelson publishers, 2000) pg. 3

[66] It is nothing more than 'cheap advice' to offer a bible verse to a person in pain and expect that because it 'worked before' it will work again. During times of incredible chaos, I have heard some of the worst *well-intentioned* biblical guidance. I am not discouraging the use of scripture, but I am asking that one be very careful as to how scripture is used in a tender time of loss.

[67] C.S. Lewis, *A Grief Observed* (New York: Bantam, 1961) pg. 11

[68] C.S. Lewis, *The Problem of Pain* (New York: HarperCollins, 1940/1996), pg. 91

[69] Lysa TerKeurst, *It's Not Supposed To Be This Way: Finding Unexpected Strength When Disappointment Leave You Shattered*, (Nashville: Thomas Nelson publishers, 2018)

Testament person, Daniel. We read in the first chapter of the book of Daniel that after being taken prisoner, Daniel *invited* his prison guard to test him! Daniel 'threw down' and challenged his prison sentry when he said, "Please *test* your servants for ten days..."[70] Warren Wiersbe has said that a faith not tested is a faith that cannot be trusted. A mature believer knows there is a redemptive purpose for pain in the overall economy of God, but having this knowledge does not make things easier. There may be an occasion, like with Daniel, where one invites God to do whatever needs to be done to realize deeper spiritual, emotional, and mental stability. I imagine that "inviting a test" might be rare, but these occasions may be the only tool that will result in lasting freedom.

The benefits of unexplainable loss

Unforeseen loss can leave a mountain of unanswered questions. Regardless of culture, ethnicity, social status, gender, or depth of spirituality, devastating loss creates more questions than answers. Pain becomes an uninvited squatter that takes up residence in our thinking, feelings, workplaces, and valued relationships. Trivializing, minimizing, or guessing why something has happened in a person's life is insensitive and disrespectful. To offer simplistic solutions to a person's emotional chaos only worsens the present heartbreak. However, I want to offer two initial benefits that come from unexplainable loss that I have seen in my own life. First, one benefit of testing is that my *head knowledge (*facts, reason, initial spirituality*)* became *heart knowledge (*deeper and more fully developed spiritual vitality*)*. My wife has said numerous times concerning my own emotional and mental development *and* limitations, "He learns slow, but he learns deep."

Many people who are converted from the neck up will eventually learn that knowledge does not guarantee resiliency or transform a life. A 'neck up' orientation to faith is ineffective during times of unexplainable loss. More than once, students said to me, "I can translate the Greek and Hebrew text and explain significant watershed events in church history, but none of this helps me work through the pain I am experiencing now." When hearing this depth of pain, my heart recalls the text, "And the Word became flesh and made his

---

[70] Daniel 1. 6,12

dwelling among us..."[71] In times of loss, people do not want our words. They need our presence. People in pain do not need a 'librarian' who offers a book to read, an 'ostrich' that puts her head in the sand, a 'banker' who dispenses a financial handout, or a 'pet owner' who tosses a bone to appease their dog.

Second, unfair experiences *revealed to me my own self-absorbed way of living*. People often *act* as if their life is on 'auto-pilot.' People running on autopilot do not have conversations with others. They deliver well-rehearsed monologues and do not realize it. When a person acts or lives without discipline and suddenly upset occurs, 'acting' turns to 'reacting.' Shallow thinking found in the life *of a believer* reveals what has been called the "Christian atheist."[72] I borrow the idea of the Christian Atheist from Craig Groeschel's book, *The Christian Atheist, Believing in God but Living as if He Doesn't Exist*.[73] A 'Christian Atheist' does not recognize their own shallow spiritual immaturity. The alleged "disciple"[74] shows *initial* signs or glimpses of spiritual maturity, but this is short-lived when adversity strikes. Paul graphically describes this expression of spirituality when writing to Titus about the people he is pastoring on the island of Crete, "They claim to know God, but their actions deny him. They are detestable, disobedient, and unfit for doing anything good."[75] Paul leaves no room for mental guesswork as to how he sees these people who call themselves *believers!*

Jesus and the pain of separation

Loss of anything of value results in pain. Scripture describes Jesus as being a "man of sorrows" and "well acquainted with grief.[76] The idea of separation is seen throughout Jesus' life, *even before he was born!*

---

[71] John 1.14, NIV translation

[72] Craig Groeschel, *The Christian Atheist, Believing in God but Living as if He Doesn't Exist*, (Grand Rapids, Zondervan, 2011). This is THE book to have in describing the reality of the functional atheist who is active in the Church today.

[73] Ibid., This is THE book to have in describing the reality of the functional Christian atheist who is active in churches today.

[74] The word, "disciple" is best translated, "learner". But as we know, Jesus' own disciples had a difficult time of grasping the lessons that Master Teacher Jesus, was laying down. On one occasion Jesus is heard saying, "Have you been with me for so long that you still do not know?" (John 14.9)

[75] Titus 1.16

[76] Isaiah 53.3

Jesus was *separated* from heaven as he came to earth as the incarnate Son of God[77]. Jesus was *separated* from the glorious realities of heaven and the presence of his heavenly father. These are examples of *temporal, relational, and eternal separation*. Jesus *separated* himself from the deceitful teachers of his day.[78] Jesus' teaching ministry can be described as 'teaching that separates.'[79] Oh, that today's pulpits would teach in such a way!

Certainly, Jesus experienced *relational separation* when his disciples abandoned him, *emotional separation* as heard from his pleas from the cross, and ultimately, *separation from life itself,* as seen in Jesus' ultimate death. Yes, Jesus was well acquainted with the concept of separation and loss.[80] Separation from things we love creates distress. Experiencing distress is part of living. Every believer needs to better acquaint themselves with the tools needed for living with people who are experiencing pain. This is not a call to counselors and pastors alone but a call to every person who sees themselves as a believer in Jesus Christ.

The Path Forward: Paul's thorn in the flesh explained

I invite the reader now to read 2 Corinthians 12. 7-10, as found below:

7 ...because of these surpassingly great revelations. Therefore, in order to keep me from becoming conceited. I was given a thorn in my flesh, a messenger of Satan to torment me. **8** I pleaded with the Lord three times to take it away from me. **9** But he said to me, "My grace is sufficient for you, for my power is made perfect in weakness." Therefore, I will boast all the more gladly about my weaknesses so that Christ's power may rest on me. **10** That is why, for Christ's sake, I delight in weaknesses, insults, hardships, persecutions, and

---

[77] Hebrews 4.15

[78] Matthew 23 is an entire chapter where Jesus rails against the Pharisees as they do not practice what they teach.

[79] I am compelled to say the ignoring of a host of subjects concerning doctrine and the practice of spiritual disciplines has resulted in spiritual malnourishment, nationwide. We are living in the days of a spiritual 'reset' where believers are being invited to be a part of Kingdom advance or, will be left behind.

[80] See, *Out From the Shadows, Biblical Counseling Found in the Story of Creation* for a complete unpacking of what I call, "separation theory" as found in scripture.

difficulties. For when I am weak, then I am strong.[81] I close this chapter by making several practical observations when explaining the need for resiliency, especially during a time of loss. Paul uses the word "thorn" more than an inconvenient splinter. Different commentators of this text say Paul's use of the word thorn is the same word to describe a stake used for torturing prisoners. Specifically, we know this "thorn" (or stake) was a "messenger from Satan."[82] By Paul identifying Satan as the source of his trouble, Paul is also saying, "I am *not* blaming God for this pain in my life." The thorn must have been a source of extreme pain, as Paul asked three times to have the thorn removed. The use of the word "torment" in verse seven implies a pain that was a repeated attack.[83]

What did Paul learn from this experience? Let's allow Paul to speak for himself. Paul said he heard the words, "My grace…"[84] This refers to Jesus's personal presence in Paul's painful situation. People in pain do not need a secondhand experience of God. People in pain need to know that God is personally involved in their circumstances. People will believe in you before they believe in your God. Game over if people in pain are not assured that the person offering help is deeply invested in their pain.

Second, the use of the word "sufficient" is understood as "more than enough."[85] Processing loss of any kind takes significant time, prayer, and practicality on the part of the helper. People in pain need the assurance that the caregiver is 'more than sufficient' to help address their pain. Over the years, I have taught my students that ministry is not 'convenience-based.' When severe loss interrupts a person's life, significant time, prayer, and resourcing are what are needed.

Third, Paul might say confession can result in God's transforming and healing presence in a person's life. The confession of pain is one spiritual discipline that can result in God's transforming power. Pain is the 'go-to' chisel in the toolbox of the Master Craftsman. The experience of pain opens the portals of heaven as a person can

---

[81] New International Version
[82] 2 Corinthians 12.7
[83] 2 Corinthians 12.7
[84] 2 Corinthians 12.8
[85] 2 Corinthians 12.9

experience God more deeply. The use of the words "I take pleasure in" is more correctly translated as "I willingly incline or position myself towards."[86] Does Paul take pleasure in this pain that came from repeated attacks? [87] Certainly not. Why would a person "lean into" this type of abuse? Paul wants his audience to know that the mean-spirited behavior he received from others did not weaken him but made him stronger because of God's grace. And let me also say one cannot be mean-spirited and be Spirit-led at the same time.

Fourth, the reality of unanswered prayer is clearly found in this passage of scripture. God did not answer Paul's prayer *the way Paul wanted*. 2 Corinthians 12 teaches God does not always remove difficulty. There will be times when God does not remove "the sea" in front of us but rather "parts it."[88] God does not always heal a life but resurrects it.[89] One reason God allows us to experience pain is so we can speak promises to those who are still in pain.[90] Paul must have taken comfort in knowing that Jesus, like himself, asked the Father three times to remove the cup of the cross from him, but Jesus still went to the cross.[91] Do you see this parallel? This persistent prayer, although not answered as either Jesus or Paul wanted, demonstrates a total reliance on the wisdom found in the perfect will of God. Yes, Jesus went to the cross with a crown of thorns on his head so that we could live our lives with a crown of empowerment on ours! I came to summarize my thoughts on this text with this personal reflection.

Whenever there has been silence or a "No" on the part of God for one request in my life, there has often been a provision in another area of my life that surpassed my original request.

God's provision was always best, even when some of my requests were short-cited or self-centered.

---

[86] 2 Corinthians 12.10
[87] 2 Corinthians 12.10
[88] Exodus 14. 19-31
[89] John 11. 1f.
[90] 2 Corinthians 1. 3-8
[91] Matthew 26.39,42

I now offer final thoughts on people and pain, through the words of Paul,

> We are like common clay jars that carry this glorious treasure within so that this immeasurable power will be seen as God's, not ours. Though we experience every kind of pressure, we're not crushed. At times, we don't know what to do, but quitting is not an option. We are persecuted by others, but God has not forsaken us. We may be knocked down, but not out. We continually share in the death of Jesus in our own bodies so that the resurrection life of Jesus will be revealed through our humanity. We consider living to mean that we are constantly being handed over to death for Jesus' sake so that the life of Jesus will be revealed through our humanity. So, then, death is at work in us, *but it releases life in you.*[92]

Paul contrasts temporary common clay jars found in the ancient world to be containers that hold the glorious presence of the heavens. Paul contrasts the images of death with resurrection, being persecuted but not forgotten, being knocked down but not out, and being pressured but not crushed. Facing such painful realities *demands* complete honesty, an honesty that recognizes and embraces the depths of a painful situation. Resistance to such honesty only feeds the imposter's voice that offers an easier escape route. Lysa Terkeurst says it this way, "...honesty finds and invites the real me to *come out, come out, wherever you are*... honesty is a suitor that is not swayed by pretending or positioning. I can try to make things better than they seem, but honesty will have nothing of it."[93] Henry Cloud, in his book

---

[92] 2 Corinthians 4. 2-12, The Passion Translation
[93] Lysa Terkeurst, *Uninvited, Living Loved When You Feel Less Than, Left Out and Lonely*. (Nashville; Thomas Nelson publishers. 2016), pg.1

Necessary Endings, says that people resist the reality that is before them because people's unresolved painful endings or losses of the past leave a person badly damaged and, therefore, unwilling to possibly experience another loss.[94]

If any of the ideas found in this chapter resonate with you, then you have joined Paul as he speaks of our lives being fragile jars of clay, persecuted but not forgotten, pressured but not crushed, and yours is a life that is learning to live with a "thorn in the flesh." There will be times in our lives when a person becomes well acquainted with a night filled with tears, but joy will come in the morning.[95] The nights can seem long, but the night will end with a glorious dawn. God bless you, dear reader.

Resilient Realties:

- o A part of resiliency is having an ongoing intentional mindset that is determined to get back up after life knocks a person down.
- o When thinking is the last action taken during heartache, heartbreak is not far behind.
- o A hard truth about trying to help a person with a victim mentality is that some people prefer victimization over liberation.
- o During times of excruciating loss, people experience a lack of peace; the purpose is questioned, and understanding the future is sheer guesswork. Overcoming emotional and mental turmoil is a process that does not come in a day, from a book, a counseling session, or a single bible passage.
- o In times of loss, people do not want our words. They need our presence.
- o When a person *acts* or lives their life without discipline, and an upset occurs, *'acting'* turns to *'reacting.'*
- o Separation from things we love creates distress. Experiencing distress is part of living. Every believer needs to better

---

[94] Henry Cloud, *Necessary Endings.* (New York: Harper Collins publishing, 2010), pg. 9
[95] Psalm 30.5

acquaint themselves with the tools needed for living with people who are experiencing pain. This is not a call to counselors and pastors alone but a call to every person who sees themselves as a believer in Jesus Christ.

- Shallow or unexamined thinking and unbiblical behavior will eventually expose a person's true nature.

- The leader during catastrophic loss must be spirit-led and not allow circumstances to dictate decision-making.

- Whenever there has been silence or a "No" on the part of God for one request in my life, there has often been a provision in another area of my life that surpassed my original request.

- One of the best practical interventions I can offer caregivers and mentors when facing a catastrophic loss is remembering that 'less is best' (I am referring to the words we speak).

- The goal of all mentoring relationships is that people become independently dependent on Christ.

- People will believe in you before they believe in your God. If people in pain are not assured that the person offering help is deeply invested in their pain, game over.

- The confession of pain is one avenue of God's transforming power. Pain is the chisel in the toolbox of the Master Craftsman. Pain is often the medium of God's transforming power.

- Whenever there has been silence or a "No" on the part of God for one request in my life, there has often been a provision in another area of my life that surpassed my original request. God's provision has always worked best, even when some of my requests were short-cited or self-centered.

CHAPTER THREE

An Unlikely Community

Kindness experienced in the community is a language that the deaf can hear, and the blind can see.
Mark Twain

Two are better than one because they have good returns for their work. If one falls down, his friend can help him up. But pity the one who has no one to help him up!
Ecclesiastes 4. 9, 10

Chapter Summary

- ➢ Surprised by community
- ➢ Community and the business world
- ➢ Community, an unlikely midwife
- ➢ Community, a place to heal

Introduction: Surprised by community

Community is a vital ingredient in a revitalized life, a dynamic ingredient that propels a person into sustained, resilient living. In chapter four, you will learn that over 400 responders surveyed ranked community as a highly valued ingredient as it relates to resilience. One false message that the COVID-19 epidemic brought to the Church was that there was now a valid reason not to be in the community. Some wrongly think their new online church experience is the best thing that has happened for them.[96] I challenge this thinking, *especially if the Church has wounded a person.* Someone who has been hurt in their church experience might say, "If you only heard my church hurt

---

[96] Two results (at least) of the COVID epidemic were the very real initial need to not meet, publicly and two, offer reasonable alternatives for not meeting, publicly. This second result or byproduct of COVID was the birth of "on-line gathering". Initially, this made sense. However, as COVID lifted (and to be sure, there would be reoccurring instances), many people chose to continue to "gather on-line" rather than meet publicly. More will be said about this, 'to gather or to not gather, this is the question', in the body of this chapter.

story..." And I might say, "I'll trade my church-hurt *stories* for yours, any day." Two key ideas concerning community need to be advanced as we begin to explore the indispensable need and value of community: (1) It is nearly impossible for a person to start over a chapter of their life without a caring community, and (2) community is not a superficial add-on to a sustained resilient life.

During my writing, I was prompted to revisit a book in my library that was given to me by a dear friend well over twenty-five years ago.[97] The book was *The Road to Daybreak* by Henri Nouwen.[98] Henri Nouwen was a Catholic priest, university scholar, psychologist, and writer, but these would only be titles, recognitions, or accomplishments. Despite his many accomplishments, Nouwen's life was also marked by tremendous internal emotional turmoil. Nouwen writes in a journal published just prior to his death

> "Everything came crashing down-my self-esteem, my energy to live and work, my sense of being loved, my hope for healing, my trust in God... everything. Here I was, a writer about the spiritual life, known as someone who loves God and gives hope to people, flat on the ground and in total darkness. What happened? I had come face to face with my own nothingness. It was as if all that had given my life meaning was pulled away, and I could see nothing in front of me but a bottomless abyss."[99]

The majority of Nouwen's personal, professional, and academic life was that of a teacher at Notre Dame, Harvard, and Yale and traveling widely for prestigious speaking engagements. Yet, Nouwen felt God calling him to leave his familiar academic and highly public surroundings in the United States and move to Canada. A life that had been lived out rather externally and publicly took a major internal detour. I pause here to offer a significant transformation principle:

---

[97] Thanks, JT. Thanks for so much more than words could ever say.
[98] Henri Nouwen, *The Road to Daybreak*. New York: Image books, 1988 (first publication)
[99] Henri Nouwen, *The Inner Voice of Love*, New York: Image Books, 1996, pg.

God often invades our settings of familiarity and comfort and puts us where we must trust Him more deeply.

Nouwen's repositioning of life, vocation, and identity placed him in a 'community' of mentally handicapped adults, a far cry from the halls of academia. Once in this highly unlikely setting, Nouwen would become a pastor to individuals who had been largely the 'cast offs' of society. Henri would live the last ten years of his life in what he referred to as "his family" and would die from a heart attack at the age of 64.[100] I believe Nouwen's heart probably broke many times while living in this community before his heart ultimately gave out. It would be from this improbable group of forgotten people that Nouwen would learn a most profound element that only community can teach, "The main question is not 'How can we hide our wounds?' so we don't have to be embarrassed, but 'How can we offer our woundedness in the service of others?'"[101] This question deserves serious consideration and is best processed *with others*.[102]

Sociologist Brene Brown echoes Nouwen's approach to life as she adds, "Owning our story can be hard but not nearly as difficult as spending our lives running from it. Embracing and sharing our inadequacies is risky, but not as dangerous as giving up on love, belonging, and joy ..."[103] If I interpret Brown correctly, if a person wants to experience authentic community, a person will need to take risks. A person who chooses to take risks in the community will be required to become deeply vulnerable, as suggested by both Nouwen and Brown. My contention is that community offers some of life's most valued treasures that cannot be experienced in the solitary life. And now we turn briefly to the community of the business world ....

---

[100] A most intimate and accurate reporting of Nouwen's life, using Nouwen's own words, can be found in the biography, *Henri Nouwen A Restless Seeking for God*, by Jurgen Beumer. I was sad when I came to the last page of this poignant re-telling of Nouwen's life. For the person unfamiliar with Nouwen's work, this is a great introduction.
[101] Henri Nouwen, *The Wounded Healer*. New York: Doubleday Books, 1972
[102] Questions that come to my mind include, "Is there an experience or event in your life that you are reluctant to talk about?" Or "Do you have an unspoken chapter in your life that has been emotionally 'left open' that others could help you, 'close'?
[103] Ibid, pg. 6

Community and the business world

If you are between the ages of 35 and 55 and want your life to have more meaning in the decades to come, read this next section carefully. I share the following statistics because they are critical for a better and healthier understanding of community. Social demographers report that people are living longer. Researchers who track college graduates report only 27% of college graduates have jobs in fields that directly apply to a major that they spent thousands of dollars to earn.[104] "Why does he include this statistic?" you might ask. As I was writing this chapter, I spoke with a former ministry student of mine who, today, works in the field of business and finance and is pursuing an MBA. He commented to me, "While I was a student of yours, I never realized that I had an interest in business and that it was in me all along. I just did not see it when I was in college." Do the math; 72% of college graduates work in a field that they could not have imagined when they were in college! A recent *Pew Research* article reports that within five years, those with an undergraduate degree in the field of religion no longer work in a church setting.[105]

The business sector records that 32% of Americans over the age of 65 are still working.[106] Because of this reported data, persons between the ages of 35 and 55 must be more keenly aware of present trends in the vocational landscape, *trends that most people do not see.* Why such an emphasis on tomorrow's culture? Researchers of today's marketplace agree a vocational reinventing of oneself is a *distinct probability, not a possibility.*[107] This 'reinvention of self' shows meaningful professional relationships (or community) are a near equal benefit when compared to the garnered paycheck. One might ask, "Does my current professional community, at least the one I am currently in, give me as much meaning and satisfaction as when I first

---

[104] *The Atlantic Monthly*, May 2013. This research was generated by the Federal Reserve Bank of New York
[105] Pew Research, December 2021
[106] Jacksonville.com marketplace, July 2017
[107] *Forbes* magazine, a recognized periodical in the business and finance sector regularly includes articles on, "Reinventing of Self for a Second Career". The reader might be interested to know that *Forbes* named the calendar year, 2023, as the "Year of Reinvention". (December, 2022)

joined this group?" In short, the authentic community can deeply reach into a person's deepest passions. And these discoveries of self, ability, and lasting joy can happen *more than once* in a person's lifetime.

<u>Now, to those *over* the age of 55</u> ... Regardless of profession, this stage of a person's life has been described by one business consulting firm as "plateauing."[108] The "plateauing" category can be described as no longer climbing or seeking professional development or advancement. Using the world of physical fitness, an analogy can be helpful here. When the body adjusts to a certain workout routine (improvement stops or slows down), a change of routine becomes necessary; a change of routine must change if the body is to continue to develop healthfully. I witnessed plateauing in the academic community, where I saw instructors nearing retirement no longer keep up with current research in their given areas of discipline. These same instructors were resistant to introducing newer and more relevant ideas in their classes. It was nearly comical to see some instructors holding onto and using 'overhead transparencies' and were slow to learn the technology that power point projection offers. I am embarrassed to say that when a student came to me back in 2000 and asked if I would consider using power point in my teaching, I said, "What is that?"

During the writing of this chapter, I met with one person in the business sector who spoke of their supervisor, over the age of 55, as "unwilling to change, consider new ideas and whose vision was focused on yesterday." I spoke with a high level administrator who commented that "working remotely" was a fad that would not last.[109] This person is badly mistaken. Mark Jobe gives an account in his book, *UNSTUCK, Out of Your Cave, Into Your Call*, that getting stuck can happen *at the age of 21!*[110] Let me also say that I have counseled with persons in their 80s who were looking for additional personal growth! *If a person is not growing, they are plateauing.* One way to protect oneself from the dangerous reality of plateauing, regardless of

---

[108] BoldCEO, September 2021
[109] This person is in for a very rude awakening.
[110] Mark Jobe, *UNSTUCK, Out of Your Cave and Into Your Call.* Chicago: Moody Press, 2014

age and vocation, is to actively engage with people who are at least ten years younger than your current age.

If the reader is close to the age of 55 and responsible for hiring new staff, it would be wise to hire people *at least* 10 to 15 years younger than yourself. Younger and forward-thinking persons enhance the life of the business community. Cautions for those over the age of 55 (if you are still reading) include the following:

- o Persons over the age of 55 frequently default to a 'no decision zone' (passive-aggressive resistance) later in life.[111]
- o Because of rapidly changing culture, people over the age of 55 do not know…what they do not know.
- o Women are an invaluable contributor to the corporate sector (this should go without saying!).
- o Working remotely has redefined business culture and is here to stay.
- o New avenues of learning (especially technology) are often seen as a threat.
- o Lifestyle and decision-making become undisciplined.
- o New potential opportunities for growth are ignored or not seriously considered.
- o A romanticized past (something seen as better than it was) is preferable when placed side by side to an unknown but possibly life-changing future.
- o The reader should know this is my SHORT list.

As I was finishing these thoughts on the over-55 age individual, I was reminded of the older film, *The Rookie*, with Denis Quaid. Quaid plays a high school baseball coach who had always had the lifelong dream of being a major league baseball player. Then, one day, opportunity comes knocking in an unlikely way. Quaid is smart enough to talk to his father, who tells him, "It is alright to do what you want to do until the time comes to do *what you were meant to do.*" BAM!!

---

[111] I could easily argue this expression of leadership is rightly called, "passive aggressive".

Community, an unlikely midwife

As I paused to think about my own personal and professional life and my own experience with resiliency, I thought, "Where would I be today if it wasn't for various communities who helped guide my professional and personal decision-making?" The larger the goal a person has, the greater the likelihood that other people will be needed to achieve the desired outcome. Very simply, the community can be the midwife that 'delivers' a person's future. Many years ago, I was privileged to attend a financial workshop with a small group of people that was led by John Maxwell.[112] In this intimate setting, I heard the following unforgettable counsel, "One is too small a number to achieve anything of significance."[113] This truth profoundly applies to the community's indispensable role in a person's resiliency. Even now, you might want to push the 'pause button' on your reading and ask, "What unaccomplished goal do I have that my heart chases after?" "Am I drawn to this idea of resiliency?" "Do I have a close friend with whom I can share the content of this book?" To ask these questions *and contact a friend* might indicate that you long for a deeper experience of community.

Allow me now a most sobering reflection and application. What I share next clearly shows how community and identity are connected. Just a few short months ago, I chose to resign from my teaching post that I had held for twenty-two years. As a tenured Associate Professor, I had job security. I did not know fully what God was asking of me except to trust Him. A person with a 'rear view mirror' approach (backward-looking) to decision-making has plateaued and would not consider doing what I chose to do. *Making idols of the past and resting in the security of the present are guaranteed ways to miss what the future offers.* When this attitude or belief system emerges, a person is beginning to die. As I moved my library from the university to our new home in the country, my books reminded me of my passion for healing, prayer, and counseling. My library became a mirror that reminded me of who I once *was*.

---

[112] John Maxwell is a highly respected leadership practitioner and has authored dozens of best-selling books on leadership.
[113] John Maxwell during a financial training workshop

While gazing into this 'mirror' (the simple task of placing books on shelves) and writing this chapter, I sensed God say to me, "Look how the years have slowly eroded strong passions that you once held so firmly in your younger years. I have missed My time with you; your voice...has become but a whisper to Me." These words were a gentle corrective. Frighteningly, I recognized I was nearing the dangerous place of having a 'plateaued' life. I journaled, "my heart is hearing what my mind could not fathom...my heart and mind are becoming one again." I was reminded of God's correction spoken to the Church in Ephesus in the book of Revelation. The reader might not know the name Ephesus means "desired one". Through John's pen, God says, "Desired one, I know your deeds, hard work, and perseverance. You have endured much... But I have this against you, you have left your first love... return to me and do the things you did at first."[114] The reading of these very words found in Revelation brought my writing to a screeching and grinding halt.

Now deeply rooted in reflective silence, the scriptural invitation "return to me and do the things you did at first" became unshakeable. I revisited the previously mentioned works of Henri Nouwen, specifically his work, *The Return of the Prodigal.*[115] This book is Nouwen's retelling of Jesus' famous parable of two lost sons, found in Luke 15. Nouwen writes, "He (the outwardly rebellious son) didn't return because of a renewed love for his father. No, he simply returned to survive. The son realized his current way of living had resulted in being empty-handed and broken-hearted."[116] Continuing on, Nouwen offers hopeful observations to those who might consider "coming home" ...

> "I am moved that the father doesn't require a pure heart before embracing us...Even if we *return* because our sins did not offer as much satisfaction as we had hoped, God will still take us back. Even if we *return* because we learned we could not make it on our own, God will still receive us. God's love does not require any

---
[114] Revelation 3.2-5
[115] Henri Nouwen, *The Return of the Prodigal*, New York: Doubleday books, 1994
[116] Henri Nouwen, *Road to Daybreak*, New York: Doubleday books, 1988, pg. 72

explanations about why we are *returning*. God is simply glad that we did."[117]

Nouwen's emphasis on "returning to the things of God" was a jarring reminder of promises that I had once made but had not fully kept. "Coming home" does not mean a person gets a free "get out of jail free" card. No, far from it! Today's cultural Christians want what is called in the academic world an 'audit.' In colleges, an audit is offered to students who attend class, get the academic information, interact with the instructor but do not do any of the assignments or take any exams. Because there is no academic accountability (through test taking and written assignments), these students experience only a limited benefit of the educational enterprise. Like the academic sector, church attendees who have spiritually plateaued do not want to be tested. Familiarity or "plateau" has become a best friend to those who approach God with a 'spiritual audit' orientation. In truth, an 'audit approach' to the community or a personal relationship with Jesus Christ will only result in a life that gets highjacked by an unseen enemy. Many Church attending persons today, and sadly, some pastors, 'audit' Jesus but do not follow him.

Two final ideas came to my attention in my period of quiet. I emphasize that these two concluding thoughts came only after I stopped writing. You would be right to say, "He got a start over during his writing!" I would also say to you that the process of resiliency often happens when we least expect it!

First, I am deeply aware some people reading this book carry with them 'church hurt.'[118] Sadly, the church community has been a place of betrayal and pain rather than healing and transformation. A host of researchers identify the signature reason younger generations leave the Church today is because 'Christians are not safe to be around.'[119] The invitation to be a part of a church community or to trust a small

---

[117] Ibid., pg. 73; I have added my own italics to alert the reader of the importance of "returning"
[118] David Kinnaman, *You Lost Me, Why Young Christians Are Leaving Church*, Grand Rapids: Baker Books, 2011
[119] David Kinnaman, *Unchristian, What a new generation really thinks of Christianity*, Grand Rapids, Baker Books, 2007

group leader is unthinkable. Church hurt results in having a chip on one's shoulder, a wound a person does not recognize, but it does. It has been said our lives are like the moon. We all have a shadow side. My best guess is that an unspoken reason you picked up this book is that you have a 'certain' longing because you sense there is more in life than you currently are experiencing. This unconscious desire is an invitation that awakens the defeatist Eeyore inside a person. The invitation to the community both frightens yet unmistakably draws a person to a greater and deeper freedom in Christ that can only be discovered in the community.

At the beginning of this chapter, I shared that I felt God taking me back to my "community memories."[120] In resolving my own painful trek that resulted in a deep mistrust of the Church (I am not saying I am totally through it yet), I was reminded of Joseph's statement to the very brothers who had hurt him when they sold him into slavery *22 years earlier*. You may know this story: famine had hit the land, and Joseph's brothers came asking for food, not knowing their brother 'held the purse strings' to the national pantry. Upon seeing Joseph, a paralyzing shock must have crossed their faces as Joseph said, "You meant evil against me, but God meant it for good…" [121]

My imagination tells me it very well may have taken Joseph twenty-two years of personal exile to heal. Years of silence may have included bouts of depression, legitimate hatred, second-guessing, and thoughts of valid victimization, not to mention retaliation. The act of betrayal, especially by a family member or close friend, does not heal overnight. Joseph's pain must have carried elements of Post-Traumatic Stress Disorder.[122] I will address the implications of this

---

[120] In a later chapter I will address the subject of "triggers", those experiences of our past that creeps up on us, uninvited memories that actually invite a person to resolve previous unresolved issues. Yes, this happened to me as I was writing this book.

[121] Genesis 50.20, ESV. I once brought a message with the title, *And Joseph Speaks*. It was many years after my incident of church hurt of which I alluded to in the above. Only by God's grace am I healed enough to "preach the word" and not merely use a pulpit to offer an unresolved rant.

[122] The American Psychiatric Association has defined Post Traumatic Stress Disorder (PTSD) as a psychiatric disorder that occurs in people who have

depth of pain in a later chapter. Long ago someone told me, "Sometimes your private "mess" needs to "age" before it becomes a public "message." This is wisdom. Now, as this chapter closes, I ask you to consider being part of an in-person community or small group. My strong contention is that the in-person community is vital to a person's life. Deep healing does not happen "online" but in God's time and with God's people. During a season of betrayal, I experienced as a very young leader, I isolated myself. During this season of incredible darkness and pain, I learned a significant lesson: God refuses to heal that which we refuse to feel.

Proverbs 3: 5-8 states, "Trust in the Lord completely, and do not rely on your own opinions. With all your heart, rely on him to guide you, and he will lead you in every decision you make. Become intimate with him in whatever you do, and he will lead you wherever you go. Don't think for a moment that you know it all, for wisdom comes when you adore him with undivided devotion and avoid everything that's wrong. Then, you will find the healing refreshment your body and Spirit long for."[123]

This text clearly teaches that healing from pain is not found in isolation, but in community. The words cited earlier, "do not rely on your own opinions" and "don't think for a moment that you knew it all," are clear invitations to return to the community. The verses above are a profound invitation to seek help and healing that can only be found in the community.

My second and closing idea comes in the form of a parable that I have titled "The Kite." There is an amazing story behind this piece of writing, and perhaps one day, our paths might cross, and I will share it with you. I will tell you this: this writing came out of a dream. I was awakened and caught in a state between consciousness and unconsciousness when the Spirit said, "Write". "What?" I asked. Only two words came, "the kite" .... I went to my upstairs study and drew a kite; I then began to write freely what is found below.

---

experienced or witnessed a traumatic event, series of events or set of circumstances.

[123] Proverbs 3. 5-8 cited in the above comes from the Passion translation

The Kite

There was once a multicolored kite. The kite loved climbing high into the sky, especially when there were crystal blue conditions. The kite enjoyed dancing as winds would swell beneath and around her as she moved across the sky. There were times when the dancing, created by gusting winds, got a little scary, but nonetheless, the kite enjoyed being a kite... *for the most part*. There was one feature of being a kite that was unpleasant, the attached string. The little kite loved the freedom of "flying," but she did not like being tethered. The kite often thought, "I know better than that old string." The kite did not realize there was a direct connection, a relationship between the attached string and her ability to fly. The kite thought she was doing her own flying. Then one day.... the string broke! It took a while, but the little kite finally crashed to the ground. The kite was overjoyed when the little boy finally found her. That night, after the boy ever so carefully placed the kite into the rafters of the darkened garage, the kite thought, "I really do need the string." Oh, there were still days when the kite would rather be in charge and 'fly on her own.' But on those days, the kite would remember the day the string broke, and it was then she would again realize the assuring safety she had when connected to the string. It was always late at night. Long after the boy had gone to bed, the little kite would let out a soft sigh as if to say, *'Tomorrow we get to fly again.'*[124]

Do you see the connection? Each of us is the kite. We crave the excitement of freedom. And like the kite, we forget there is a relationship between the string's tension and our ability to reach 'higher heights' in our lives. I offer a final promise: *resiliency knows*

---

[124] This writing comes with a very special shout to out to a very brave friend who allowed me into their life. YOU know who you are, you are a hero to me!

that no one ever flies alone. I do not know if it is the risk that comes with any relationship that keeps a person from seeking community. Perhaps it is the need to be in control because there was a time when safety was sacrificed. The wound of betrayal leaves a person asking, "Will I ever find a safe connecting place?" Or "Is the real connection with others a reality?" These are real questions and concerns that deserve to be answered. This book seeks to provide those answers! In case you have not noticed, the journey of resiliency has started. The string is being connected... let's fly!

Resilient realities ...

- The more significant the reboot a person faces, the greater the likelihood that help from a caring community will be needed.
- God often invades our settings of familiarity and places us where we must trust Him more deeply.
- If a person is to experience an authentic community, one must take risks.
- Community can be the midwife that 'delivers' a person's future.
- When community ceases to be a part of a person's life, the loss of identity is not far behind.
- To make idols of the past and rest in the security of the present are guaranteed ways to miss what the future could possibly offer.
- Reboots can happen when we least expect them.
- If a person is not growing, they are plateauing.
- God refuses to heal that which we refuse to feel.
- Rebooted lives know that no one ever flies alone.

CHAPTER FOUR

YOU SAID IT!

Chapter Summary

- ➤ The story behind the survey
- ➤ Description of the survey
- ➤ The survey
- ➤ The process of data retrieval and interpretation
- ➤ Final Field Data
- ➤ Field Data Observation Worksheet
- ➤ Final interpretation of surveys

The story behind the survey

In chapter six, I mention I was part of a small group of professionals that gathered from across the country via Zoom. Our initial purpose for the meeting was to idea share about the dynamics of trauma. Over the weeks, as our Zoomed discussions continued, the term "resiliency" repeatedly surfaced. Having written and published a counseling book previously[125] and working in higher education at the time, I was tasked to create a proposal that would address the theme of resiliency.

I strongly felt a survey would be of great help and lend greater credibility and practicality to the project. The *purpose* of this survey would be to gain people's experiences and beliefs and how they might respond when faced with a trauma of some kind. It is important to note that a 'self-reporting' survey like this would be entirely subjective. Subjective findings are based upon a person's personal feelings, opinions, and experiences and are not impartial or facts. To be sure, subjectivity has both its strengths and weaknesses.

---

[125] Bill Effler, *Out From the Shadows, Biblical Counseling Revealed in the Story of Creation.* (Bloomington: Westbow Press, a division of Thomas Nelson. 2014)

The *end goal* of the survey would be to include the results from the participants in whatever form the research might eventually take. As I researched and wrote, I was able to create a simple twelve-question survey that the reader can find later in this chapter. Wide-ranging data was taken from people in all walks of life (i.e., age, gender, relational status, education). This survey revealed a more complete understanding of resiliency. Participants of this national survey were mostly, but not solely, people active in a local church. The accompanying interpretation proved to be an invaluable and fascinating experience that lent itself to a more complete understanding of resiliency. Lastly, of those taking the survey, only 4% of participants found the survey difficult to complete or understand.

The created survey was distributed and taken by nearly 400 people. From this number, 351 surveys were successfully recorded and later interpreted by myself and a research assistant. Later, a twelve-week 'pilot group' using the yet-to-be-published book as a guide shared their lives and beliefs about trauma and resiliency. This pilot group of more than 20 participants verified what we had suspected. Week by week, we saw an increasing openness in our participants as they freely talked about their experiences with loss and their desire to live more resiliently.

Description of survey

1) A copy of the survey is provided for the reader, and the reader is free to take the survey if they wish.

2) Age, gender, relational status, and education were all factors considered in this survey.

3) Additionally, the survey targeted four areas that either foster or hinder resiliency. These four areas are:

⇒ Thinking: the value or capacity a person places on analyzing information and logically assembling this information for the purpose of problem-solving.

⇒ Feeling: the value or ability a person places on the capacity to emotionally self-regulate, monitor, and/or utilize emotions during times of decision-making.

⇒ Acceptance: the value or ability to acknowledge reality (either recognize what is before a person or ignore, discount, or not accept reality).

⇒ Community: the value or preference a person places in relationships; a person's desire to connect with people or work individually.

4) A scale measuring a participant's resiliency is provided below.

43 - 48: Highly resilient... YOU can be a resiliency coach to others!

38 - 42: Above average resiliency... celebrate with someone.

33 - 37: Average resiliency ... there is room for growth.

28 - 32: Situationally resilient ... factors in your life impact your resiliency.

Below 28: Share your questionnaire results with a trusted friend.

Resiliency Questionnaire

To the right of each statement place an "x" in the box which is most appropriate for you. After answering the questions, total up the number of "x's" in each column and place that total under each column at the bottom of the page. Multiply the number under each column by the number at the top of each column. For example, if there are four boxes checked under "disagree," write "4" under that column, then multiply four by 1 (the number at the top of the column). Once you have the four column numbers, add the numbers up to receive a <u>total score</u>. After completion, a "Total Scoring" sheet is on the back of this page that provides a description and explanation of the questionnaire and all resiliency levels.

Place a "x" in the appropriate column	Strongly Disagree **1**	Disagree **2**	Agree **3**	Strongly Agree **4**
1. I can accept a disappointment fairly quickly and move on.				
2. I learned in my home growing up healthy ways of relating to others.				
3. I carefully research all of my options before making a decision.				
4. I do not allow negativity to affect my emotions for very long.				
5. I make decisions based on facts rather than imagination.				
6. I am energized by new ideas.				
7. I can monitor my emotions easily.				

8. I know I will not accomplish every goal I set, and this is part of life.				
9. I enjoy group success as much as I enjoy individual success.				
10. I stay focused when faced with disappointment.				
11. I do not allow people or circumstances to determine my decision making.				
12. I have often heard I am a people person.				
Column Totals x # at top:	___ x 1 = ___	___ x 2 = ___	___ x 3 = ___	___ x ___ = ___

Column 1 ____ + Column 2 ____ + Column 3 ____ + Column 4 ____ = _____ Total score

Please check the appropriate boxes:

Age: ☐ Under 18 ☐ 18-35 ☐ 36-50

☐ 51-65 ☐ Over 65

Gender: ☐ Male ☐ Female

Relationship Status:

☐ Single ☐ Married ☐ Divorced ☐ Widowed

Was this survey clear and understandable? Yes ____ No ____

Level of Education:

☐ High School ☐ College ☐ Post-College ☐ Other

Survey results:

43-48: Highly Resilient… you can be a resiliency coach to others!

38-42: Above average resiliency…celebrate with someone.

33-37: Average resiliency… there is room for growth.

28-32: Situationally resilient…factors in your life impact your resiliency.

Below 28: Share your questionnaire results with a friend you trust.

The process of data retrieval and interpretation

1. Surveys were distributed, taken, and gathered from participants. Time was spent formatting, recording, and organizing the raw numbers. No interpretation was considered at this stage.
2. A "Final Field Data" document, using the raw numbers (data), was created that shows the recorded scores from the surveys. Again, no final interpretation of the numbers was done at this time.
3. After the actual raw numbers were organized in a simple and understandable format, the results (data) were extensively reviewed by me (Bill), and assistant, Ms. Shannon Riese.[126] At this stage, *individual general* observations were made and recorded, but no interpretation of the observations was recorded.
4. Following the *initial review* of the data, which took place over several meetings, preliminary observations and conclusions were individually recorded.
5. A "Final Field Data Observation Worksheet" was created for the possible use of people who may, one day, be a part of a "resiliency group." This worksheet can be seen as a tool to help people better understand the survey. This worksheet is provided for the reader.
6. After a final review of numerical data from survey participants and individual narrative interpretation by evaluators, a "Final Summary Observation The document" was created using both the raw scores and observations by evaluators. This document is also provided for the reader.

---

[126] Ms. Shannon Riese holds a Master of Science degree in Marriage and Family Therapy and currently works in a residential treatment facility in Florida. Shannon's area of interest and focus is with sexual trauma and abuse.

FINAL FIELD DATA[127]

A total of 351 surveys were *successfully* completed and evaluated. Approximately 10% of the total amount of surveys collected could not be used because they were not filled out completely or correctly. 15 out of 351 completed surveys reported the survey was not clear and or understandable (4.2%).

Ages Surveyed	Number Surveyed	Average Total Score	Highest Area of Evaluation	Lowest Area of Evaluation
18-35	125	34.48	Community	Thinking
36-50	92	34.75	Feeling	Acceptance
51-65	80	34.88	Feeling	Community
Over 65	54	36.05	Community	Thinking

Area of Evaluation	Female	Male
Average Score	34.298	36.485
Highest Area of Evaluation	Community	Feeling
Lowest Area of Evaluation	Acceptance	Community
Maximum Overall Score	46	45
Minimum Overall Score	22	23

---

[127] See "description of survey" to better understand these raw scores.

Genders Surveyed	Female	Male
Number Surveyed	188	163
Scored 38 or Higher	30	56
Scored 43 or Higher	21	39
Scored 32 or Lower	121	84

Relational Status	Number Surveyed	Average Total Score	Highest Area of Evaluation	Lowest Area of Evaluation
Married	205	34.686	Feeling	Acceptance
Single	80	35.224	Feeling	Thinking
Divorced	51	35.235	Community	Feeling
Widowed	15	32.625	Community	Thinking

Field Data Observation Worksheet

Created by Dr. Bill Effler & research assistant Shannon Riese

In addition to identifying gender, age, education, and relational status, the data analysis addressing resiliency targeted four specific areas. A low score in any one of these categories can potentially hinder resiliency. These four areas are thinking, feeling, acceptance, and community.

1) The **"thinking"** category places the value a person places on logic and reasoning when faced with the decision to 'start over' or consider change.
2) The **"emotions"** category indicates a person's ability or inability to self-regulate or manage emotional responses when considering a change.
3) The **"acceptance"** category targets a person's ability or inability to have a realistic view of a given situation or reality.
4) The **"community"** category is the value placed on a person's ability and/or desire to readily connect with others during times of decision-making.

An initial look at the raw data resulted in a sampling of statements and questions by Effler and Riese.

- Does a higher or lower score in *any of the four above categories, either help or hinder a person as they seek to move through a situation where a change* is needed?
- What does a lower/higher score in the "acceptance" category imply?

    The question could be asked, "How might a lack of acceptance impact a person's ability to live resiliently and 'move on' with their life quickly?"

- "Do you think persons of faith should have greater or lesser difficulty accepting reality than non-churched people?"

Based on what criteria should a person of faith have a greater ability to make changes in their life, where a clear and needed change is called for?

- "Does emotional regulation, mental stability, or spiritual maturity factor at all when considering the subject of resiliency and 'moving on' with one's life?

  How might a person's emotional well-being (feelings), mental stability (thought life), and/or
  spiritual orientation (faith) factor into the need to make a necessary change in life?

- In looking specifically at the data in the 'community' category, what are your observations?

  Do you think the 2020 COVID-19 reality impacted the Church's view of 'community'? Has the COVID-19 reality legitimized for people a rationale for no longer meeting with others?

Final Summary Observations on Field Data

The field survey on resiliency was specifically designed to evaluate four targeted areas that either lent themselves to resiliency or prevented a person from becoming resilient. These four areas were selected based on research from multiple scholarly articles. Research routinely showed that "thinking (mental reasoning), feeling (emotional control), acceptance (to hear or see reality), and community (relationships)" were four significant factors found in the practice of resilience or the ability to quickly overcome a hardship or difficulty.[128]

Again, the "Thinking" category applies to a person's ability to apply logic and reasoning when faced with a problem or disappointment and move on to a successful resolution. The "Emotions" category is the ability to self-regulate or discipline emotional response in problem-solving and healthfully access and utilize emotions to problem-solve or face a disappointment. The "Acceptance" category applies to a person's *ready* ability to have a realistic view, acknowledge, receive, hear, or come into agreement with established truth. "The "Community" category applies to the value placed in connecting or relating to others and the value personal relationships play when faced with a potential setback.

After reviewing the raw data, the following summary observations were made. No specific order, preference, or weight apply to the following:

- Age distinctions: Several observations can be made here.

~ *No age group* scored themselves as being "highly resilient." What does this say about contemporary culture? One could say 'life challenges' occur in all age groups and that disappointment visits all age categories.

~ There is something to be said about *cognitive development being the lowest score* for both those in the 18-35 category and those over

---

[128] The reader may want to review the variety of definitions of resilience that is found at the front of the book.

the age of 65. Both the youngest and oldest groups did not score or value "thinking" as a primary indicator of resilient living. One might ask, "How might hasty decision-making come into play in a person's life?" And "Might these age groups live more resiliently if "thinking" were to be more readily used in decision-making?"

~ Ages 36-64 rank "feeling" as their primary value when it comes to resiliency. If "thinking" is rated low, as seen above, and therefore results in life challenges. It seems logical that disappointment would result in a variety of feelings. The 36-64 age group seems to draw on or utilize their emotional abilities and resources to live resiliently. Again, using "feelings" to navigate hardship is admirable, but equally, the other three tested areas should also be considered when facing hardship.

- A *lower score* in the "acceptance" category indicates people tend to escape, deny, or at least have difficulty facing reality. The question might be asked, "How might a lack of acceptance (or seeing reality) impact a person's ability to live resiliently or "Come back from disappointment' *quickly*?" A second question might be, "Do people of faith or those with a religious orientation have greater difficulty with 'accepting reality than non-churched people?" Last, ages 36-50 scored "acceptance" as their lowest resiliency indicator of the four indicators being tested. What does this lower score of "acceptance" seem to indicate of those who are presently in their 'vocational years'? How might a lack of acceptance prevent someone from coming back after disappointment? Or, how might greater acceptance enable a 'faster comeback' after a trial of any kind?

- A *higher score* in the "community" category was found in both the youngest group. (18-35) and the oldest category (over 65). What does this say about these stages or stations of life? The data also shows persons between 36-64 did not score or see the relational connection as a priority. Why is this? Are those persons, in their 'vocational years,' too busy raising a family or getting established in their careers? Also, divorced and widowed responders placed community as their *primary resilient indicator*. The reader is encouraged to review or read the chapter on community again.

- Relational status comparative: The data shows married people scored an overall *lower resiliency score* (34.6) than both single (35.2) and divorced people (35.2). One might think marriage would lend itself to a higher resiliency score, but the data shows this is not true. Also, *married people* scored "acceptance" (to see and hear reality) as the *lowest resilient indicator,* whereas *single people* highly value "emotions" in resilient living.
- Gender comparatives: Again, several observations can be made in this category.

~ Females value or rank "community" as their *highest value* in resilient living, whereas males value "community" as their *lowest value* in resilient living. What does this large difference say about the genders?

~ Females dramatically placed themselves in *the lowest resiliency category* (121 responders) while 84 males placed themselves in the lowest resiliency category. Are females more critical of themselves than males?

~ Males self-scored themselves as being 'highly resilient (56), whereas only 38 females scored themselves as highly resilient. Do males have an inflated view of their abilities?

~ One possible interpretation of the category of 'male and female resiliency.' Based upon these limited findings, is that females are more critical of themselves as compared to males. If these findings carry any weight at all, men need to be aware of this reality. And women, in a different fashion, should be aware of how men view themselves.

43-48: Highly Resilient… you can be a resiliency coach to others!

38-42: Above average resiliency…celebrate with someone.

33-37: Average resiliency… there is room for growth.

28-32: Situationally resilient … factors in your life impact your resiliency.

Below 28: Share your questionnaire results with a friend you trust.

Part 2: Resilience and How it Works

Part Two: Resilience and How it Works

Chapter Five: Rewiring Your Brain

Chapter Six: Rejecting Your Triggers

Chapter Seven: Releasing Your Past

Chapter Eight: Reclaiming Your Future

CHAPTER FIVE

Rewiring Your Brain

The left brain runs at the speed of words; the right brain runs at the speed of joy.
Dr. Jim Wilder

The American Institute of Health estimates that 75–90 percent of all visits to primary care physicians are attributed to our thought life.
Dr. Caroline Leaf

Trauma is not about an event that took place in the past but an imprint on the brain that has ongoing consequences.
Dr. Bessel Van Der Kolk

Chapter Summary

- ➢ You and your brain
- ➢ A brain story
- ➢ Rewiring the brain
- ➢ The brain and attitude
- ➢ The brain and conflict

Introduction

The brain plays a significant role in living resiliently. Long before a person has a feeling or is prompted to act in any way, the brain has already been engaged. Yes, the brain functions long before a person feels or thinks *anything*![129] Specifically, this chapter identifies the role brain plays during conflict and how the brain can help address and reduce conflict and help promote resilient living.

---

[129] *University of Sydney* research documents that various structures or segments in the brain, working together, contour the brain in such a way to accomplish whatever is trying to be achieved. October 2019

One of the joys of research and writing is discovering that other writers and researchers have already gone before you! A very recent article on brain development and chemistry stated the brain's role of "self-sculpting" enables a person to live intentionally and helps self-monitor or police thoughts.[130] This self-monitoring results in greater positivity in relationships, reduces stress and ultimately results in adopting *a more resilient life*. This article went on to say

> "Your brain changes with every new thought, new thing you learn, and new experience you have. This plastic, complex, and fascinating organ can be our ally when it comes to preventing and treating endless conditions. One of the greatest experts in the field of cerebral plasticity is undoubtedly Dr. Álvaro Pascual-Leone. He's a researcher, professor, and Associate Dean of the Clinical and Translational Science Center at Harvard Medical School.... According to Professor Pascual-Leone, 'We must understand that it's up to us to "sculpt" our own brain to make it an ally instead of an enemy. Surrounding ourselves with caring and genuine people, being curious and receptive, thinking positively, and reducing the impact of stress will undoubtedly allow us to improve our health and well-being.'"[131]

Understanding how the brain functions is not as complex as some might imagine. Weighing approximately three pounds, the brain's two general sides or parts function as a unit. Housed within these two compartments are many functioning parts; there is no single most important part. This chapter will introduce only a limited number of

---

[130] Exploring the Mind, "Your Brain Can Heal You", November 2021
[131] Ibid, Exploring the Mind, "Your Brain Can Heal You", November 2021

these parts. Research reveals that people use both sides of their brain every day. Some people are naturally more creative (right-side brain activity), while others are more analytical (left-side brain activity).

As we begin this chapter, a comparative analogy of brain activity with the making of a motion picture film is helpful. The brain is a 'camera' that is turned on by a life event or experience. Each side of the brain, both left and right, 'talks to one another' about the picture (life event) that is being viewed and recorded. Working as a unit, the two sides of the brain create a 'script' (beliefs and memories) of the recorded event. Yet, in the 'motion picture recording process', something interesting happens: the brain compartmentalizes or stores data. What started out as a 'moving motion picture' project becomes distinct moments captured in 'still shots' (recorded memories).

In considering both the 'moving picture' and the 'still shot' metaphors about the brain, the entirety of Proverbs 27 offers very practical counsel about our beliefs or thoughts: *be careful* about sharing one's thoughts with a "fool" (v.9), *apply* all that has been heard (v.12), and finally, the *mental discipline* one engages in will result in a faithful life (v.19).[132] Proverbs 23.7 offers specific instruction concerning our thoughts and behavior in the familiar text, "as a man *thinks* in his heart, so is he." This single verse shows internal thought life powerfully influences character.[133] One might ask, 'How does a person become better at disciplining their brain?' The biblical character, the Apostle Paul, specifically answers this question, "Keep your thoughts continually fixed on all that is authentic and real, honorable and admirable, beautiful and respectful, pure and holy, merciful and kind. Fasten your thoughts on every glorious work of God, praising him always, and put into practice all that you have heard and seen in me…"[134]

A very partial and selective overview of the brain is found below. A story that follows will illustrate how five portions of the brain were

---

[132] One might pause now to ask, 'What do you think about?' 'Do I have someone to share my inner most thoughts with?' 'Do I regularly apply all that God's word instructs?' And, 'Does my thought life create, the best version of me?'

[133] In this chapter the words "mind" and "heart" are intentionally interchanged, as both seem to carry equal importance and weight.

[134] Philippians 4. 7-9. *The Passion translation*

activated in the lives of three characters described in the story. Clear and practical application of the recorded story will be offered.

General: You and your brain

Left brain - the left half or hemisphere of the brain is generally aligned for tasks that involve logic (i.e., science, mathematics, judgment, goal setting). Decision-making is largely processed in a very analytical way. A left-brain-dominated individual prefers to be taught something rather than 'learn by doing.' Lawyers, mathematicians, administrators, and doctors would be examples of left-brain-oriented careers.

Right brain - the right half or hemisphere of the brain is generally seen as more intuitive (i.e., having a 'gut feeling,' abstract, creative). Decision-making could be described as 'taking a journey' rather than 'arriving at a destination.' Right-brain-dominated persons prefer to be shown how to do something rather than read about it in a book or be taught in a classroom. Artists, chefs, counselors, actors, and ministers are examples of right-brained careers.

Summary: Brain researchers tell us the two sides of the brain are very different, each with its own emphasis, value, and orientation. The exact functions of the varying parts of the brain vary from person to person based on multiple factors (i.e., a person's upbringing/family, birth order, a life event, or gender). The short story below illustrates how multiple parts of the brain, each functioning uniquely, are critical in potentially resolving a conflict.

A Contemporary Brain Story

Readers are encouraged to read the story below more than once. The story will be interpreted by identifying five specific ways the brain functioned or reacted in the story. A diagram and practical applications will explain how the brain might have reacted to this event.

A painter was hired to do work on a private residence. At the end of the day the painter used the hose and water from the house next door to carefully clean his brushes. The next-door neighbor saw the painter using his hose and water and came outside. The painter became the target of high-pitched yelling arm waving and experienced a tirade of unrestrained vulgarity. The emotional outburst escalated. The painter never said a word. The painter's silence seemed to further agitate the neighbor, resulting in total out-of-control behavior. The man who had hired the painter came outside to offer help. The outburst continued as though the offer of help was never heard. The look of his neighbor's bright red face was frightening; tension raced through the homeowner's body. The owner of the house had never seen this behavior from his neighbor before and genuinely wondered if this would result in a total physical altercation.

Specific: Five specific names and functions of the brain with application to the story

Hypothalamus – the brain's general 'control center' in the inner most part of the brain that manages chemical 'messages' (experiences/events) and keeps the body balanced. The hypothalamus helps manage multiple functions of a person's body (heart rate, blood pressure, and hormone production).

Application: The hysterical explosion in both the painter's and homeowner's hypothalamus initially recorded the event. But, the hypothalamus did not interpret the event.

Amygdala – is the brain's *'alarm clock'* that recognizes external stimuli and releases neurons throughout the body. Neurons are 'information carriers' to other cells, muscles, or parts of the brain. The phrases, 'fight, flight, freeze or frown', are all ways of decoding the amygdala's message sending capacity. The amygdala also has the ability to translate events or experiences into memories.

Application: As the rant *began*, the painter's and homeowner's amygdala immediately 'sounded an alarm' to the entire brain and throughout their bodies. It is as if the amygdala might have said, "If you are not awake now, you need to be!"

The cerebral cortex- is the brain's *'911 emergency control center'* where fact-finding abilities gather and process a given situation. This forwardmost portion of the brain manages thinking, feeling, personality, and decision-making and stores memories.

Application: The cerebral cortex of the upset neighbor, the painter, and the homeowner *initially* gathered facts about the situation. Initial feelings begin to develop, but the analysis of the event has yet to reach a complete conclusion.

Mirror neurons - are the brain's *'caregivers or first responders'* that explain why and what a person feels about an event or experience. Mirror neurons in the brain stir feelings in people and can release empathy, stimulate fear, affect muscle control, and frame a person's thought life, as recorded in the story.

Application: Mirror neurons told the painter and the homeowner that 'something is very wrong.' The activity of mirror neurons creates a 'fight, flight, freeze, or frown' response in both the painter and the homeowner. *On the flip side,* the agitated next-door neighbor might have had *little to no mirror neuron activity*. Research shows people with significant mental health challenges (i.e., commit murder with no sense of remorse) have little to no evidence of mirror neuron (ability to feel) activity.[135]

Neuronal pathways – are the *'streets' that the brain's emergency responders travel on.* When an event happens, paths are created throughout the brain for mirror neurons to travel on. When traveled frequently, the brain's 'streets or pathways' A neuronal pathway can be 'redirected' or changed, much like a GPS redirects the route of a car.[136] This redirection of thinking can change the brain's chemical format, resulting in decreased anxiety because an alternative route or way of approaching any situation has been taken.[137]

---

[135] Studies show that people with severe mental health issues can switch the empathy-oriented function of their brains on and off at will. The most deviant of criminals often show a greatly reduced ability to empathize with others, including their victims. Jeffery Dahmer, the convicted serial murderer of the 1990s, is an example of this behavior. See BBC News, the Scientific Reporter, July 2013

[136] This type of redirection is referenced in the mental health community as, "clinical behavioral therapy" and is commonly used in treating anxiety disorder.
[137] Research in pornography addiction shows the use of pornography creates neuro pathways in the brain. The addiction becomes stronger and frequency increases because new pathways of more graphic images are needed to gain the chemical release that results in the pleasure that the addict seeks.

Application: The hypothalamus 'recorded' the initial 'tirade event' and the amygdala 'sounded the alarm' concerning the upset neighbor. Then, the cerebral cortex used its 'fact-finding abilities to communicate' to the 'caregivers or first responders' (mirror neurons). The first responders then 'traveled the neuronal pathways' in hopes of getting the brain back into balance or, restore the brain to a place of calm.

Diagramming the story from a brain activity orientation[138]

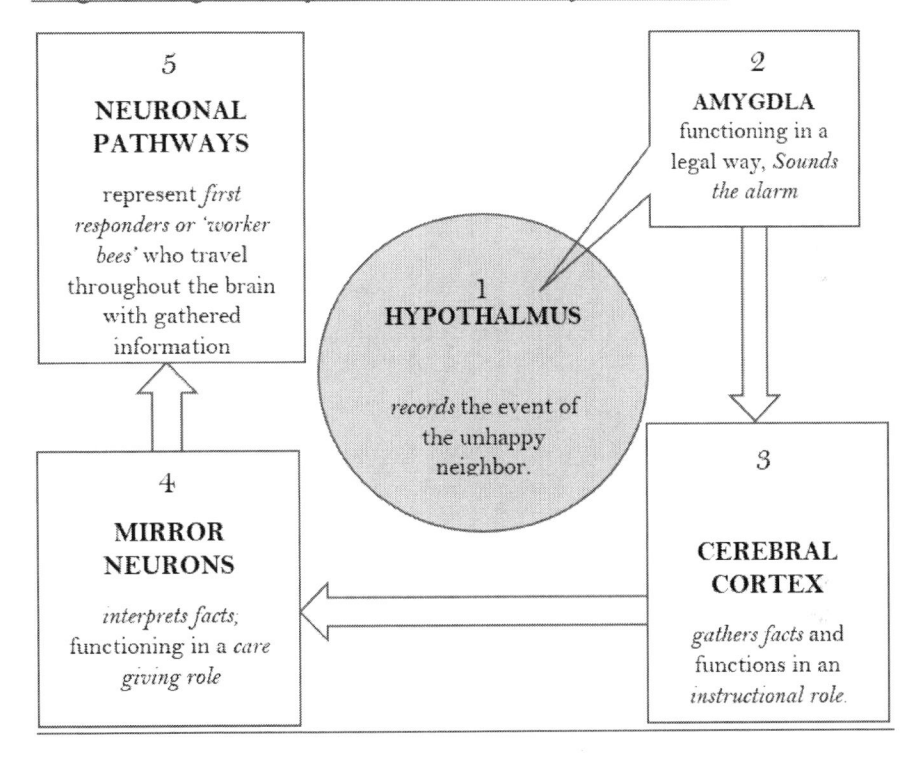

5
NEURONAL PATHWAYS
represent *first responders or 'worker bees'* who travel throughout the brain with gathered information

2
AMYGDLA
functioning in a legal way, *Sounds the alarm*

1
HYPOTHALMUS
records the event of the unhappy neighbor.

4
MIRROR NEURONS
interprets facts; functioning in a *care giving role*

3
CEREBRAL CORTEX
gathers facts and functions in an *instructional role.*

Story Summary: the brain and resiliency

After writing the above short scenario (*I was the homeowner that had hired the painter!*) and offering an application to brain functioning, I asked, "How might a brain get 'restarted' given a similar situation?" Two important ideas directly relate to 'rewiring

---

[138] A small group discussion of the story, while looking at the above diagram could bring added clarification to those still unclear about the brain and its many functions.

our brains' during a conflict: *(1) a person's attitude during a challenging situation is paramount, and (2) because of the culture of increasing hostility in which we live, one must know that the brain becomes impaired or 'hurt' when it witnesses or experiences intimidating aggression or heightened negativity.* Brain researchers have long held that the brain functions at its best when it is in a 'state of calm' and that, the brain is always seeking to get to this preferred prenatal state.[139]

The brain and attitude

The first influential book on the brain I was introduced to was *"Who Switched Off My Brain?*' by neuroscientist Caroline Leaf.[140] Dr. Leaf initially engages her readers by describing the anatomy of thought with this opening idea: *"Behavior starts with a thought. Thoughts stimulate emotions, resulting in attitude and, finally, behavior is produced."*[141] Leaf contends that long before a person ever *does a*nything, a thought is registered. Although it may be a deeply buried subconscious thought, a thought exists. Leaf continues by saying, "…thought life, attitudes, habits, and emotions are largely responsible for mental and physical health… Your thoughts can de-stress you, making you more clever, calm, and in control of your emotions, *or they can do just the opposit*e. The choice is yours." [142]

Leaf might say thoughts fuel emotions, but an attitude drives a person to action. If thoughts are the 'fuel' that leads to the flash of action, 'attitude' is the small, unchecked, flickering flame that creates or stimulates the roaring fire. *Attitude is the internalized version of feeling and thinking that eventually becomes recognized external behavior.*

Paul writes to the people living in Philippi, saying, "Do nothing out of selfish ambition or vain conceit, but in humility consider others better than yourselves. Each of you should look not only to your own

---

[139] This 'state of calm' (or absence of) can be viewed on YouTube under the brief video, "Still Face experiment".
[140] Caroline Leaf, *Who Switched Off My Brain?* (Dallas: Thomas Nelson), 2007
[141] Ibid, pg.1. I added underlining to emphasize Leaf's equation: thought, feeling, attitude and behavior/action.
[142] Ibid, pg. 5,8. Italics added for emphasis

interests but also to the interests of others."[143] Paul summarizes his thinking about attitude by saying, "Your attitude should be the same as that of Christ Jesus."[144] Concerning attitude, Paul writes to the church at Ephesus saying, "You were taught, with regard to your former way of life, to put off your old self, which is being corrupted by its deceitful desires and *be made new in the attitude of your minds*; and put on the new self, created to be like God in true righteousness and holiness."[145] A careful linguistic study of the word 'attitude' shows there is a connection or relatedness of 'attitude' with being a servant to others and/or a willingness to suffer. In the case of either service or suffering, a person's internal attitude will certainly be tested.

A brief Old Testament case study contrasts *the opposite of* what Paul describes in his writing to the Ephesians and the Philippians. The prophet *Jonah's disobedience to the calling and work of God is an example of having a bad attitude.* God called Jonah to warn Nineveh that their sins had come to God's attention and that God would deal with them. Instead of doing what God asked, Jonah runs in the opposite direction and flees to Tarshish. His bad attitude led to disobedience. Jonah finally relents *for a season* and does what God had originally commanded. Jonah's attitude change, as seen in Jonah 2 and 3, is short-lived. In Jonah 4, Jonah's bad attitude returns as he criticizes God for saving the lives of 120,000 people. Jonah also has self-destructive thoughts concerning his own life.[146] The case study of Jonah leaves us with serious questions: If Jonah has God's Spirit, how does a godly person lose sight of God's call? Will God accept people with a Jonah attitude? Has God needed to be as patient with me, as God was patient with Jonah?

In his book, "Enemies of the Heart," Andy Stanley identifies four *negative attitudes* that fuel a person's behavior. Certainly, there are many more, but these four negative attitudes offer a clear framework to better understand negative attitudes. I summarize Stanley's thinking with the following: the *attitude of guilt* says, "I owe you." A person

---

[143] Philippians 2. 3,4
[144] Philippians 3.5
[145] Ephesians 4. 22-24
[146] Jonah 4.9

recognizes they have done something wrong and, therefore, "owe" or will regretfully repay what is owed. Second, *the attitude of anger* says, "You owe me" because 'you have taken something from me.' Third, *the attitude of greed* says, "I owe me." This negative attitude carries with it an element of entitlement because "I should be rewarded." Very simply, greed is not content with what it has but, *only wants more* of what it already has gained. And finally, *the attitude of jealousy* sees what others have and says, 'Because others have "X," I should have it too.' A most toxic aspect of this last attitude is when a person becomes jealous of another person, and the other person loses something of significance. The person with the 'bad attitude' celebrates the other person's loss.

Concerning attitude, one must know that God's ultimate goal for His children is not comfort but rather the transformation of minds and ultimate godliness. The Christlike attitude that Paul speaks of begins with the transformation of our minds and does not bow to the attitudes and values of the world (Romans 12. 1,2). Paul comments that attitude *outwardly reflects* the internal fruit of the Spirit (Galatians 5. 22,23) and is *inwardly motivated* by sacrificial love (1 Corinthians 13).

The brain and conflict: escaping "enemy mode"[147]

Neurotheologian[148] Dr. Jim Wilder believes the church today has relegated individual character transformation to a much lesser priority as comparted to other aspects or ministries of the church. Wilder argues convincingly that the Enlightenment altered the way people view themselves. A central message of the Enlightenment was that people should be granted individual freedom; this freedom would eventually oppose established doctrines of the Church. Wilder writes, "Reason and skepticism have replaced God's Word as the path to knowledge and fulfillment… many Christian leaders agreed that our minds were the most important aspect of our humanity yet...The

---

[147] The term, "enemy mode" was coined by Jim Wilder and Ray Woolridge in their book, *Escaping Enemy Mode.* (Chicago: Northfield publishing) 2023. This term will be explained in our reading.

[148] Jim Wilder holds a PhD in clinical psychology and an MA in theology. Bringing together the disciplines of psychology and theology Wilder has used his extensive counseling experience and research of the brain to offer keen insight on decision making, and healthy Christian living.

proliferation of denominational splits and the ongoing failure of Christian leaders point to an over-reliance on espousing right beliefs while neglecting maturity."[149] And further Wilder writes, "Pastors were primarily prepared for preaching positions through education, not character formation. Like their pastors, most Christians possess truth but are not trained how to love well."[150]

In their book, *"Escaping Enemy Mode,"* Jim Wilder and Ray Woolridge describe an altered state of the brain, a near replica of my neighbor's behavior in the earlier story. They refer to this altered and unhealthy state of brain functioning as "enemy mode." Enemy mode favors rational and cognitive thinking over *faith*. To escape enemy mode requires the recognition that we live in a culture of hate, and if not hate, then certainly, extreme hostility. Escaping enemy mode requires one to identify signature signs found in the brain that signal enemy mode is 'alive and well.' *General characteristics* of a brain contaminated by enemy mode include the following beliefs and behaviors....[151]

- Sees other people as the enemy
- Wants others to 'lose'
- Has no compassion for anyone else's opinion.
- Cannot discern when others are trying to help
- Lives with self-justified anger
- Sees people as objects and not people
- Believes no one is on 'their side'
- Will attack or withdraw from people who could be of help
- Enlists or persuades others to help them in their attack
- Emotions and speech can easily and quickly escalate
- An unresolved past can quickly get a person's brain into enemy mode

Three specific enemy mode expressions[152]

---

[149] Jim Wilder and Michel Hendricks, *The Other Half of Church*. (Chicago: Moody Press. 2020). Pg. 45
[150] Ibid, pg. 46 This last quote could create wonderful small group discussion.
[151] Ibid, pgs. 21-40
[152] Ibid, pgs. 48-58 offers a more detailed look while pages 59-126 offer an in depth understanding of enemy mode.

Wilder and Woolridge identify three specific expressions or portraits of people whose brains largely function in enemy mode. Below are three introductory enemy mode profiles offered by Wilder and Woolridge. One way of maximizing this portion of reading is to think of persons in your life who demonstrate the signs in each category.

1) Simple enemy mode

- Not interested in what others are saying
- Feels ignored, manipulated, or misunderstood
- Answer questions with abrupt responses
- Is rule-based; focuses on procedure and policy that benefits them
- Has few relational skills or social sensitivity

2) Stupid enemy mode

- They are attention seekers.
- Their voice is the loudest and the last heard.
- Initially promised one thing only to take it back.
- Often feel overwhelmed or out of control; I live with a lot of drama.
- Withhold information that they know others would benefit from having.
- They capitalize on other people's vulnerabilities.
- They cause damage to things that are of value to others.

3) Intelligent enemy mode

- They are above the rules.
- They make their own rules.
- Ignore other established rules.
- Do not value loyalty or the values of others.
- People are seen with a lower status and are to blame for a situation.
- Being in control is more important than being in a relationship.
- Humiliation or discrediting others is used to gain a preferred position.
- They consciously work to hide their true selves.

- Winning is their only true priority.
- There is an odd disconnection between ethical talk and ethical action.

In a previous chapter, it was acknowledged that we live in a spiritual state of conflict or spiritual warfare. In his book, *The God-Shaped Brain*, psychiatrist Timothy Jennings writes,

> "The Bible says we are in a battle, with weapons that demolish arguments and pretensions that are opposed to God, and *our thoughts are to be harmonized with Christ*. The battlefield on which the war between Christ and Satan is fought is *in the mind*. I take the position that it is not only legitimate but also vitally necessary to take Scripture as a whole and use it to obtain the fullest revelation of God's character."[153] [i]

Jennings' application of scripture to the reality of spiritual warfare and a person's thought life is well balanced. Through the study and reflection of the Word of God, working together with a better understanding of brain chemistry, we can escape what Wilder and Woolridge call enemy mode. *When our true selves are anchored in healthy relational attachments (personal relationships) and a 'peace that passes understanding'*[154] *is achieved (mental clarity), our brain is provided with stability that enables a person to function at its absolute optimum.* Wilder and Woolridge summarize their contribution concerning "enemy mode" in the following way,

> "Identity is assembled stage by stage, starting at the bottom of the brain and working up. We reinvent who we are many times a second. If this process in the right side of the brain fails, our identity stays incomplete and unstable. Enemy mode is likely…Our main objective is keeping our brain running in a stable relational condition."[155]

---

[153] Timothy Jennings, *The God Shaped Brain*. (Downers Grove: Baker books) 2013, pg. 12. My italics added for emphasis
[154] Philippians 4. 5-7
[155] Jim Wilder and Ray Woolridge, *Escaping Enemy Mode*. (Chicago: Northfield publishing) 2023. Pgs. 261-263

The outset of this chapter states that understanding our brains is not as complex as some think. Yet, life experiences and the adjoining chemicals released in the brain can easily sabotage our minds and behaviors. Despite the complexities of both life and science, good and evil, thinking and feeling, I conclude this chapter with the assuring words of Thomas Merton, "Quit keeping score and surrender yourself with all your sinfulness to God who sees neither the score nor the scorekeeper but only his child redeemed by Christ."[156]

Resilient Realities:

- Some people are naturally more creative (right side of the brain), while others are more analytical (left side).
- "Behavior starts with a thought. Thoughts stimulate emotions which then result in attitude and finally produce behavior."
- Two ideas directly relate to 'rebooting our brains' during a conflict: (1) the impact and influence of a person's attitude during a challenging situation and (2) because of a culture of increasing hostility in which we live, one must know that the brain becomes impaired or 'hurt' when it witnesses, or experiences intimidating aggression or encounters extreme negativity.
- When our true selves are anchored in healthy relational attachments (personal relationships) and a 'peace that passes understanding' is achieved (mental clarity), our brain is provided with stability that enables a person to function at its absolute optimum.

---

[156] Thomas Merton, *Merton's Place of the Heart* (Notre Dame: Ave Maria Press, 1978), pg. 33

CHAPTER SIX

Rejecting Your Triggers

Whatever is triggering you is on you.
Richie Norton

Triggers are unconscious internal meteorites that, when released in the brain, explode and disrupt present conscious thought life.

A man without self-control is like a city broken into and left without walls.
Proverbs 25.28 ESV

Most triggers come from a literal experience in the past that 'pops up,' or surprises a person, putting them in an emotional freefall.

Chapter Summary

- ➢ An introduction to triggers
- ➢ Indicators of being triggered
- ➢ The process of being triggered
- ➢ Triggers and emotions
- ➢ Triggers and anger
- ➢ A tool for rejecting personal triggers

Introduction: What is a trigger?

The study group that I was a part of (which I have mentioned earlier) which studied traumatic experiences regularly came back to the subject of resiliency. The question was asked, "What keeps a person from living resiliently?" There are many roadblocks to resilient living, but the word "trigger" seemed to take on particular interest and have heightened value for our group. "Trigger" refers to spoken words or non-verbal prompts that activate the subconscious mind.[157] Being

---

[157] It might be beneficial for the reader to review Chapter Five, "Rewiring the Brain".

triggered is most frequently an *overreaction* by a person because an *unrecognized and unresolved* experience has been 'set off.' The proverbial 'you've pushed my buttons' applies to getting triggered. The force or strength of an emotional reaction (sadness, fear, anxiety, regret) verifies that a person is being triggered. In short, when a person gets *hysterical* (overreacting to a situation), something *historical* lurks in the subconscious world. If a person can recognize that their reaction to their external world has been triggered or provoked by an internal recorded reality, inner peace can be restored.

However, not all triggers are negative. A person can be positively moved when reminded of an event or person that brings back a positive memory. An example might be hearing a song that was played at the first concert one attended; hearing the song will take a person back in time.[158] Still, the word trigger, most commonly is used to describe a response to something that produces unwanted feelings or thoughts. *It is more than safe to say that nearly everyone has triggers. Most triggers come from a literal experience in the past that 'pops up' or surprises a person, putting them in an emotional freefall.* One way a person can know if they are being triggered is by what they are feeling *in the moment*. For example, if a person *suddenly* has an emotional reaction (i.e., anger, fear, anxiety, and positive exhilaration) because of something they see or a memory of the past 'pops up,' a trigger most likely occurred. At the outset, I offer this reminder, *"Let the peace of Christ rule in your heart..."*.[159] And, *"... may the Lord of peace himself grant you peace in every circumstance..."* [160]

Indicators of being triggered

If triggers in people are a common reality, one might ask, "How do I know if what I am thinking *in the present moment* is connected to an unresolved *past* experience?" Let me say here: triggers are easier to recognize than explain. There is an unlimited number of items that can trigger a person. Below, I offer a short list of examples that could

---

[158] For me, it would be my first Carol King concert that I attended. Many times, when I hear any number of her songs, I am back in the early 1970s... yup, I am an old dude!
[159] Colossians 3.15
[160] 2 Thessalonians 3.16

indicate if a person is being triggered.[161] Evidence that a person may be experiencing a "trigger" can include:

1) <u>A person's reaction</u> to something that has been said. Say Mary offers to help Lucas with something, but Lucas declines the offer. Mary might feel, 'Shut down.' Mary's feelings may have to do with Lucas' response, but this also may be a trigger that Mary has been previously rejected.

2) <u>Procrastination</u> is a sign of being triggered. A person fears they may fail at attempting something they have formerly tried or perhaps never tried. Fear of failure *triggers* avoidance.

> When someone is triggered, there is a strong *internal uncomfortable reaction* to an *external factor.* Some of these internal responses include panic, feeling overwhelmed, withdrawal or various expressions of acting out. Triggers are commonly rooted in past and unprocessed hurtful experiences. *I remind the reader* to protect a person, the brain is forever on the lookout for signs that signal possible threat of harm.

3) <u>General feelings of mistrust or uncertainty</u> are potential signs of being triggered. Because a person has been *previously* disappointed in the past, a present situation serves as a reminder of an unresolved experience. In a very real sense, the past *is not* the past. The past setting creates an unwillingness to move forward in the present. One comment that serves as an example might be, "It was a bummer last time. It surely won't be any different now."

4) <u>Feeling controlled (particularly by a strong personality)</u> is a possible trigger. A current experience of being told what to do (particularly a voice of authority) recreates former feelings of anxiety, apprehension, and panic. These feelings often stem from a prior experience with someone with a similar personality.

<u>The following three items are the three most common examples that a person has been triggered.</u>

---

[161] There are certainly many more examples of triggers than the ones listed. I have only provided illustrations or cases that I have personally seen or experienced.

5) <u>Anger,</u> particularly an irrational outburst, is a clear sign that a person has been triggered by something in the past. Once again, the emotional outburst could be due to any number of events or experiences.

6) <u>A sudden or what appears to be an irrational action.</u> This trigger happens when a person feels threatened. The triggered person physically removes themselves from a setting or relationship because the present situation has activated a past unresolved reality. I have counseled numerous people who, after visiting a church and sitting down, experienced profound dread and panic. These feelings happened because it was in a prior church setting that they had been abused.

7) <u>Re-experiencing or remembering a past event in the present</u> is perhaps the clearest indicator that a person has been triggered. This is an example of post-traumatic stress disorder.[162]

The process of being triggered

The following is a three-step process or explanation of being triggered. <u>First,</u> the brain is stimulated or prompted with an automatic thought that comes flooding into a person's mind. I previously cited Caroline Leaf commenting, "all behavior has its origin in a person's thought life." Most of these automatic thoughts are anxiety-producing and unwanted.[163] <u>Second,</u> instantaneously, the automatic thought produces an emotional and, often, chemical reaction in the brain. An example of an emotional reaction is having a panic attack.[164] A tangled

---

[162] Post-traumatic stress disorder (PTSD) is an anxiety disorder that develops in some people who have
  experienced or been through a shocking, frightening, or dangerous event. Originally studied as it related to
  returning veterans of the armed forces, this disorder is applied to many aspects of daily living.

[163] Concerning automatic thoughts, Dr. Daniel Amen has coined the
term, Automatic Negative Thoughts (ANTS). A person that demonstrates "ants" has chronic cynical, sarcastic, or rampant negativity that comes to a person in a most uninvited way. Often, these cognitive biases try to convince a person that something is true, when it is not.

[164] A panic attack is a brief and, at times for a longer length of time, of intense anxiety. Signs of a panic attack include elevated heartbeat, shortness of breath and muscle tension.

web of emotions is the predictable outcome when a person's past is suddenly awakened. And third, a choice must be made whether to grapple with the unwanted thought or ignore it. When considering a past 'pop-up,' it is important to remember that memories are fallible; over time, specific and important details about an event tend to become distorted.

The above triggering process is greatly impacted by what is called 'emotional intelligence.'[165] "EI or EQ" (both designations are used) is the ability to recognize and regulate positive and negative emotions. All emotions create physical and neurological pathways to feelings, problem-solving, and productive living.[166] Our national survey in the previous chapter identified emotions or feelings as one tool people draw on to bounce back productively when a disappointment occurs. There are both redeeming and perplexing notions concerning emotional regulation that the reader should consider. Below is a sampling of research on the topic of emotional intelligence. Emotional intelligence:[167]

- Is more dominant and influential than facts.
- It is the 'go to' lens through which a person *initially* views life (reality or not!).
- Stays with a person longer than rational or logical (left brain) facts.
- Often convinces a person of a false reality and
- can prevent a person from discovering the actual truth that can set them free.

To develop healthier emotional intelligence and lessen the potential of being triggered, a person can follow the "ABCD" roadmap below.

---

[165] This brief section on emotional intelligence is meant to be only introductory in nature. EQ is just as valuable as IQ and helps a person with self-management, self-awareness, socially appropriate behavior, and relational management. For further help consider, *The EQ Edge: Emotional Intelligence and Your Edge* by Steven Stein and Howard Book.

[166] A review of Chapter Five, "Rewiring Your Brain", or seeking the guidance through one of the books mentioned in this chapter, could be very helpful.

[167] A second practical and helpful source concerning emotional intelligence is found in *Positive Psychology, Theories of Emotional Intelligence Explained.* There are multiple resources in this area, found online.

Positivepsychology.com/team/heather-craig/. January 19, 2019

Awareness of feelings (emotions) when they *first appear*

Beliefs that are directly tied to a given situation

Choices are made based upon clarity of feelings and established facts

Do. This is the action step or what a person chooses to do.

This "ABCD" roadmap is an example of what professional clinicians refer to as, cognitive behavioral therapy and is frequently utilized in helping people process panic disorder, social anxiety disorder, and separation anxiety and help in identifying feelings.[168] A large segment of our population is *confused* about their feelings and, therefore, struggle to make *healthy choices*. One suggestion to caregivers who help people in pain is to begin by exploring a person's beliefs about what is of concern to the seeker. Problem-solving, beginning with *beliefs,* is a preferable starting place because, as stated earlier, most actions take place because beliefs fuel emotional responses. In helping people in pain, I often ask, "What do you think *exactly* happened when ….?" This question can uncover a false sense of reality, and the seeker comes to discover this themselves. The most powerful and long-lasting discoveries a person will ever obtain come from themselves.

Triggers and emotions

Triggers activate a wide spectrum of emotions. There is no set approach or 'magic wand' when it comes to the removal of triggers. Keep in mind that triggers can also be beneficial as they are a type of amygdala or alarm clock whose goal is to ensure safety.[169] Once aroused, emotional triggers (i.e., fear, anxiety, beliefs, memory) send an alert to various parts of the brain that transmit or send a message there is a possible threat to peace.

---

[168] Many online versions of what is called, 'the feelings wheel' exist. I have given a physical copy of this document to people in counseling to help people identify their feelings. Seeing this diagram proves to be helpful for the people who have difficulty in identifying their feelings. A small group exercise using the 'feelings wheel' can prove to be very beneficial to promote valuable small group discussion.

[169] If the term 'amygdala' is foreign to the reader, please review the previous chapter on the brain.

Two key ideas are important: (1) *critical awareness of* both feelings and thoughts helps manage triggers, and (2) having an *initial ability to respond* to feelings helps a person better cope with triggers.[170] In the case of severe trauma (a topic beyond our present study), caregivers, pastors, and counselors should know there are varying degrees or levels of trauma.[171] Very briefly, the more significant the trauma or painful experience, the greater the likelihood the emotions will be 'wounded' or negatively impacted; the impacted or distressed emotions will eventually and unexpectedly surface.[172]

I now purposefully turn to God's role in a person's pain and alleviating personal triggers.

Psalm 40. 1-3 reads

> I waited and waited and waited some more, patiently, knowing God would come through for me. Then, at last, he bent down and listened to my cry. He stooped down to lift me out of danger from the desolate pit I was in, out of the muddy mess I had fallen into. Now, he's lifted me up into a firm, secure place and steadied me while I walk along his ascending path. A new song for a new day rises in me every time I think about how he breaks through for me! Ecstatic praise pours out of my mouth until everyone hears how God has set me free. Many will see his miracles; they'll stand in awe of God and fall in love with him![173]

---

[170] I use the term emotional regulation, the ability to self-control one's emotional responses to others, to describe a person's ready ability to control their emotional responses.

[171] Research on trauma shows there are varying categories of trauma, ranging from acute (single event), chronic (prolonged or repeated event) and complex (severe, childhood, witnessing a violent act) trauma.

[172] In the case of severe or complex trauma, an inexperienced or non-trained person should quickly seek to refer the wounded person to a trained professional.

[173] Psalm 40. 1-3, The Passion translation

This psalm assures the reader that God *listens* to His people; "…he bent down and listened to my cry." God is *active*: "He stooped down to lift me out of danger from the desolate pit I was in…!" God will *deliver* His people to a place of security, *"...* he's lifted me up into a firm, secure place and steadied me while I walk along his ascending path." And last, God's active role in a person's deliverance *will be evidence to others* of the goodness and greatness of God, "…everyone hears how God has set me free. Many will see his miracles, stand in awe of God, and fall in love with him!"

Before leaving the subject of triggers and emotions, I offer my own simple diagram of five basic emotions. A host of practitioners have their own way of seeing emotions, but for the purpose of this printed volume, I have chosen the following interpretation. Awareness of these five basic emotions and knowing how to harness them can be extremely helpful when mentoring a 'triggered person.' Below is a diagram of the five most basic emotions and how they develop.[174]

OUR FIVE BASIC EMOTIONS

Awareness	SAD	GLAD	MAD	BAD	HAD
Very aware 10	ALONE IGNORED HOPELESS	AWARE THANKFUL EXCITED VALUED	HOSTILE CRITICAL VENGFUL	FEARFUL DISGUST ASHAMED	ANGER INFERIOR FEAR
Somewhat 5 aware					
Little Awareness 3	APATHETIC DEPRESSED LOST	PROUD FULFILLED	JEALOUS ANNOYED	GUILT EXCUSE BLAME	REGRET ANXIOUS HELPLESS

---

[174] The chart provided could be distributed and discussed in a small group setting.

Triggers and the emotion of anger

In a previous chapter, "hostility" was used to describe today's culture. If this cultural analysis is even partially correct, the *trigger of anger* must be addressed. Unprocessed or unhealthy expressions of anger prevent a person from experiencing a resilient life. A display of deep and engrained anger is a profound sign of being triggered. Introductory observations about anger are made below, followed by a comparison between godly and ungodly anger.[175] No further comments regarding anger are made. Readers are simply invited to seriously and honestly consider these introductory observations and the offered comparative categories.

General observations about anger ~

- People do not 'do' anger well.
- Anger is a God-given emotion that must be acknowledged and managed.
- Anger commonly comes with an explanation, but it is seldom good.
- Unrecognized anger is one short step away from hatred or murder (Genesis 4. 1-4)
- One sign of Christian maturity is self-control (Proverbs 29.11)
- We can begin to control our anger by controlling our thinking (2 Corinthians 10.5)
- A heart filled with anger is a heart looking to be paid back for a perceived injustice.
- A person's desired payback for injustice is often greater than the actual offense.

And now, our comparisons ...

Godly anger	Ungodly anger
Clear and specific	Lacks clarity and is often general
Truth is understood	Falsehoods or lack of reality are held

---

[175] The subject of anger is a 'must' topic to discuss when considering resiliency. Reading through and discussing the introductory observations and the comparisons of godly and ungodly anger could benefit people, greatly.

Godly anger	Ungodly anger
Constructive results	Destructive results
Is motivated by love	Driven by pride and accusation
Is self-controlled & Reactive	Lacks control
Seeks restoration and a future	Winning is more important than the relationship

A tool for rejecting triggers

STEP 1 – STOP

At the first indication or recognition that peace is leaving a person, one needs to "stop" *immediately*.

Reminder: *The brain places a high value on peace (or calm) and seeks peace "24/7"*. The ability to stop oneself when peace is leaving is a difficult discipline to practice. A scriptural reminder is helpful here, "cast your anxieties upon the Lord, for he cares for you."[176] A practical *first step* in restoring calm to the brain is to *begin the day* with the Lord. The psalmist writes, "O God, you are my God; *early* will I seek You; my soul thirsts for you; my flesh longs for you in a dry and thirsty land where there is no water."[177] A *second step* in this 'stopping step' is to reflect upon the over 60 verses in the bible that refer to God as never leaving or forsaking His people."[178] A *third step* to restore peace and reject triggers is to spend time with trusted people who have displayed safety and offer non-judgmental help. Especially as it relates to anger, time spent within the community of faith is important. There is a certain type of healing that is experienced in 'alone time' with God and a different type of healing experienced while being with other believers; a person needs *both*.[179]

---

[176] 1 Peter 5.7
[177] Psalm 63.1 NKJV
[178] This promise from God is found in both the Old Testament (Deuteronomy 31.6; Joshua 1.5) and in the New Testament (Matthew 28.20; John 14.18; Roans 8.31).
[179] An entire chapter was devoted to the importance of community or, time spent with people. For the person who has significant 'trust issues', the decision to be in

STEP 2 – START

A person who has "stopped" (or at least *significantly* slowed down) is increasingly able to recognize the presence of peace *and when peace is threatened*. When a person slow themselves down, they can begin to "start" to explore what is robbing them of peace. Again, a trigger is a searchlight or a reminder that illuminates something to a person. One cannot practice the "starting step" until they have first stopped their brains from running all over them!

Jesus taught that "truth sets us free."[180] To be set free from things that enslave a person requires a *deep cut* before freedom is experienced. The first step in cutting a person free from the past involves purging falsehoods and distortions that have been spoken over a person. An example of an *external message* I have heard many times is, "Your father was _____, and you are just like him." This spoken falsehood is really a 'curse.'[181] Accepting the truth of what God thinks about a person is powerful and can radically free a person from their painful past. A second idea to consider in setting a person free from their past **is** to explore the possibility of any *internal* vows or promises the person has made *about themselves*. Statements like, "I will never trust another person, ever again," is a self-proclaiming a vow or promise that must be renounced. Examples of toxic vows or promises made during a time of extreme conflict may include, "I have to be perfect before God accepts me" or "I am damaged goods. This is as good as life will ever get," or, "This is too difficult, and I just can't do it." These, too, must be identified and renounced.

A third and final thought I offer on starting a new life and being 'cut free" from the past is associated with relationships. People who have had many past relationships find it difficult to 'bond.' or be joined by anybody because their own relational journey has resulted in severe fragmentation.

---

community could be one of the most significant decisions a person could ever make.
[180] John 8.32
[181] Prince, Derek. *Curses, Cause and Cure.* (Dublin: Whitiker House publishing)

The fragmentation I speak of goes far beyond a person having 'commitment issues.' Today, there is much talk about "trauma bonding." Trauma bonding describes a relationship that exists or is based on trauma or pain. Trauma bonding finds meaning in a relationship based on pain rather than promise. This is very much an increasing reality, in our day. Allow me an example. I prayed for a woman once who had been under the care of a psychiatrist for many years and had also been hospitalized. She said to me, "I just do not know who I am." After hearing a portion of her story, I realized this woman's reality was based on her 'giving herself away' to so many men that she was right in saying, "I don't know who I am." I prayed that all the 'parts of her' she had chosen to give away would be returned to her. After prayer, she spoke of an incredible peace that had enveloped her. I reminded her that one of the names of God is "Prince of Peace."[182] Later that same week, while speaking at another conference, I saw the woman again, but this time, she was with her psychiatrist. He asked me, "What did you say to her?" In her presence, I explained to him that because she had given herself away to many men, she was quite right in saying she no longer "knew herself." And so, I prayed that she would "get back" that which she had given away. The woman's psychiatrist simply shook his head in unbelief. (This was quite funny to me).

I pause here to reflect on key passages from the Apostle Paul that offer hope for anyone who seeks to "start again." What might have been Paul's secret to overcoming his past? In what is believed to be his first written letter, Paul referred to himself as "the least of the apostles."[183] In what was most likely one of Paul's last letters, he described himself as the "worst of sinners."[184] *Paul was well aware of his past but would not be controlled by it.* Paul's possible secret to overcoming his past may be found in the following words, "But one thing I do: Forgetting what is behind and reaching forward to what is ahead, I pursue as my goal the prize promised by God's heavenly call in Christ Jesus." In a summary statement of his own resilience, Paul declares But we have this treasure in jars of clay to show that this all-surpassing power is

---

[182] Isaiah 9.6
[183] 1 Corinthians 15.8
[184] 1 Timothy 1.15

from God and not from us. ⁸ We are hard pressed on every side but not crushed; perplexed, but not in despair; ⁹ persecuted, but not abandoned; struck down, but not destroyed. ¹⁰ We always carry around in our body the death of Jesus so that the life of Jesus may also be revealed in our body. ¹¹ For we who are alive are always being given over to death for Jesus' sake so that his life may also be revealed in our mortal body. ¹² So then, death is at work in us, but life is at work in you.[185]

And finally, Paul was keenly aware of his own inadequacies as he wrote,

> Therefore, I will boast all the more gladly of my weaknesses so that the power of Christ may rest upon me. For the sake of Christ, then, I am content with weaknesses, insults, hardships, persecutions, and calamities. For when I am weak, then I am strong.[186]

To conclude this section on "starting," I remind readers that when Jesus saw (or sees today!) a person genuinely *seeking to start their life over again,* Jesus did not blame, accuse, or condemn.

Consider the way Jesus treated the woman caught in adultery (John 8. 1-11), the Samaritan woman (John 4. 1-42), Thomas and his wavering faith (John 20), Peter and his multiple denials of having never known Jesus (John 21. 15-19), and Saul, the religious legalist who murdered believers (Acts 7).

Jesus' ministry was a ministry of love, mercy, and compassion (Matthew 9.36; 14.14; 15.32; 20.34). As members of God's reconciling presence in the world (2 Corinthians 5.20), our job is to free people from guilt, not heap more on them. An experienced pastor will tell you that most people who are deeply seeking help have confessed to God repeatedly their failures but have not experienced freedom for some unknown reason. The best example of biblical restoration is Jesus restoring his and Peter's broken relationship. Jesus did not focus on Peter's failures but rather on God's willingness to

---
[185] 2 Corinthians 4. 7-12
[186] 2 Corinthians 12. 9,10

accept Peter as he was. Concerning God understanding our shortcomings and loving us anyway, David Seamands writes, "God understands what it is like to be a human being. Because of the incarnation, His ultimate identification with us in our sufferings, God now fully knows and understands, not simply from factual omniscience but from actual experience."[187]

STEP 3 – RECEIVE

God's heart leans *towards* those who are far away from Him.[188] The distance, attitude, or length of time away from God does not matter to God. God still offers help; where there is help, there is always hope. Caregivers and mentors of hurting people must remember those who live apart from God frequently have a difficult time receiving undeserved grace. It is not uncommon for people to believe they have in some way disqualified themselves from God's extravagant love. I remind the reader here of the common destructive reality that inner vows or lies play in the quest for a 'second chance.' God's promise, as spoken through the prophet Micah, tells us, *"You will again have compassion on us; you will tread our sins underfoot and hurl all our iniquities into the depths of the sea."*[189]

Self-condemned people are not helped by further condemnation. However, it is up to the seeker to ultimately "come to their senses"[190] and accept what God offers. Again, I underscore the hard reality that trusting and accepting the extravagant love of God can be very, very difficult for a person caught in the crosshairs of self-condemnation. Allow me to illustrate. As previously mentioned, Jesus tells the story of two sons. Both sons squandered their inheritance. The younger son was on foolish living, and the older son had a 'works or performance' belief system that kept him in his own self-imposed 'far country.' Again, I come back to scripture when knowing how to reject triggers.

Jesus teaches in John 14.27 that we do not need to be troubled or afraid, but rather, we can choose to accept God's peace while caught

---

[187] David Seamands, *Healing of Memories* (Wheaton: Illinois: Victor books, 1985) Pg. 54
[188] Luke 15.20
[189] Micah 7.9
[190] Luke 15.17

in the throes of anxiety. And last, "For everyone who asks receives, the one seeks finds; and to the one who knocks, the door will be opened."[191]

STEP 4 – REPEAT

My own journey to healing through God's Spirit has taught me resilient living is not a 'one and done' exercise. I say this to introduce "Step 4 - Repeat". I invite the reader to turn to Luke 24 in your bible or bible app on your phone. This story clearly illustrates the necessity of "repeat." The context of the story that Luke tells follows the resurrection of Jesus. Two travelers meet the resurrected Jesus while on their journey, yet they do not initially recognize him. In this travelogue, told only by Luke, Jesus gives an overview of the Hebrew scriptures to the two men concerning the Messiah's life and death. Why does Jesus "repeat" or retell what the scriptures say about the Messiah to the travelers? It is easy to know facts or forget facts and miss the truth.

A *first "repeat" principle* in Luke's story is that it is possible for God to 'show up' and not recognize his presence. Luke indicates that the travelers, at some level, are people of "faith," as they can tell a*bout* Jesus' life, ministry, and death (Luke 24. 18-21). The travelers must have heard of the women's testimony of seeing the resurrected Jesus (Luke 24. 9-12), but they did not believe. Was this a gender issue? Could they have thought, "Believe a woman, come on now?" Was it a case of pious pride showing through? Like the travelers, a person can know about Jesus, hear miraculous stories as told by others, and not know God. A *second observation* from the traveler's story is that God meets people while they are on their way somewhere. The story records that the longer the travelers were with Jesus when it came to part ways, the travelers wanted Jesus to stay with them. A clear indicator of the resilient life is that resilient people will want as much of the Presence of God as they can get (Luke 24. 28-30).

An *important third 'repeat' idea* must be observed. It is within a community, sharing a meal together and having the scriptures

---

[191] Matthew 7.8

faithfully opened, that the traveler's hearts, in the words of John Wesley, were "strangely warmed" (Luke 24. 31-35). Here in this story, we perhaps see the possible removal of the trigger of unbelief. Luke records a *most significant fourth 'repeat' point*. The travelers transitioned from being individuals who were holders of information (hearing) to the formation (believing) and, ultimately, transformation, as evidenced in their bringing their testimony back to those in Jerusalem (Luke 24. 34, 35).

But the lesson of "repeat" is not over. Luke records sometime later (Luke 24. 36-43) Jesus makes yet another appearance, and *again*, the band of brothers *do not* recognize Jesus! (Luke 24. 37) And like before, Jesus opens the scriptures to them (Luke 24. 44-48) with the hope of removing the trigger of unbelief. The practiced principle of "repeat" includes significant facts. God knows we are *(1) slow to learn, (2) prone to not recognize the activity of God, (3) people who need other people, and (4) like the travelers that needed to have a lesson 'repeated'; a 'repeat' is often part of the journey of faith.*

The story of the traveler's experience teaches the significant lessons found in the life of anyone who is on their way to resilient living:

1) A person can know facts but not the truth.
2) Personal transformation often takes place when we are on our way somewhere.
3) A person can be surprised by the presence of God.
4) Resilient living is very discernable.
5) Some people will not believe our story of transformation.
6) Deep and lasting change will be grounded in scripture.
7) The transformed life has a strong desire to share their story with others.

I close this chapter with a declaration of God offered by Brennan Manning. This declaration, written by a former alcoholic, has everything to do with "rejecting our triggers," especially the trigger of 'self-condemnation' …

"…I know your whole life story. I know every skeleton in your closet. I know every moment of sin, shame, dishonesty, and degraded love that has darkened your past. Right now, I know your shallow faith, your feeble prayer life, and your inconsistent discipleship. And my word to you is this: *I dare you to trust that I love you just as you are and not as you should be.*"[192]

Resilient Realities:

- A trigger can include almost any number of things, but in the end, if a person can recognize that an internal recorded reality has triggered their perceptions of their external world, inner peace can be restored.
- When a person gets hysterical, there is usually something historical beneath the surface.
- Nearly everyone has triggers. The majority of triggers come from an experience in the past that comes as a 'pop up' or surprise and takes a person into an emotional prison.
- When considering a past 'pop,' it is important to remember that memories are fallible; over time, specific and important details about an experience tend to become distorted.
- Unprocessed or unhealthy expressions of anger prevent a person from experiencing a resilient life.
- The brain is forever on the lookout for peace (or calm) and things that disrupt peace. The brain seeks peace "24/7".
- One can only practice the "starting step" after first stopping their brains from running all over them!
- It is easy to know facts or forget facts and miss the truth.
- God knows we are (1) slow to learn, (2) prone to not recognize the activity of God, (3) people who need other people and (4) like the travelers, we too will learn that having a lesson 'repeated' is part of the journey of faith.

---

[192] Brennan Manning, *The Ragamuffin Gospel.* Colorado Springs: Multnomah Books. 1990. My italics added for emphasis

CHAPTER SEVEN

Releasing Your Past

One of the most painful parts about releasing a past relationship is realizing that the other person already has.

"God has done for us what we do not deserve. He therefore wants us to do for others what they do not deserve."
R.T. Kendall

Releasing the past is an agonizing process, but not as painful as choosing to let the past rule your present life.
"Where a man's wound is, there you will find his genius."
Robert Bly

Chapter summary

- ➢ The dirty dozen signs of an unreleased past
- ➢ An exercise in releasing the past
- ➢ Renewal for the wounded warrior
- ➢ Three stages of personal wounding
- ➢ Forgiveness: a critical key to release the past
- ➢ The gift of choice

Introduction: Releasing my past

This chapter was profoundly the most difficult chapter for me to write. You will find 'flashes of the academic' but more commonly, unvarnished narrative.

I first experienced trauma in my first year of graduate school; a *personal* experience that I thought could never happen, did. A little over two years later, in my first position as a new pastor, I was blindsided by an equally painful *professional* situation. The personal and professional traumas were equally devastating. I would not be the only victim; my family would become collateral damage. My emotional and mental carnage would take years to clean up. I learned, only years later, that my wife watching my own internal chaos, suffered in silence, not knowing what to say. Even today, I suffer a degree of pain for the torture I put my family through. More than twenty years after these accounts transpired, I had a 'beach experience' that I have written in my former book, *Out From the Shadows,*

> "I began my late afternoon saunter on the beach, walking directly into the sun; the South Carolinian breezes gently cooled my face. As I glanced back, the footprints that had marked my steps had been eclipsed by the incoming tide. I also saw my shadow. It seemed so big. My heart became imprisoned by an imperfect replica, an emotional stalker that would not let me go. That day taught me that if I walk facing the "Light," I will not see my shadow. Conversely, when I *turn away from* the "Light," I will be viciously reminded of who I once was. That day, I came to realize that only "Light" can provide direction, point to a desired destination, and silence the Accuser's voice that maligns the true meaning and existence of who I am in Christ. Of greater significance, my 'shadow' is not how God sees me. My life's journey, in part, has been to learn how to come "out from the shadows"...[193]

People are often left speechless when I tell these two stories of my shadow experience. A counselor helped me to see I needed to make the deliberate choice to release the persons and settings that had devasted my life. This decision would become non-negotiable. It was in a season of counseling and recovery I wrote, "Don't fake it till you

---

[193] Effler, Bill. *Out From the Shadows, Biblical Counseling Revealed in the Story of Creation.* (Bloomington: Westbow Press, 2014. Pg. xxi)

make it. Face it till you beat it and chase it back to hell where it belongs!"

The whole idea of resiliency is based on believing that all is not well. If, indeed, all was well, there would be no need for resiliency. Many want a better life without understanding or admitting that something is wrong. A person may not necessarily be in the wrong or bad, but what has happened to a person has detoured their life. Perhaps NOTHING is a greater threat to resiliency and experiencing inner peace than the temptation to ignore present pain and hold onto the past. Choosing to release the pain of the past is an intentional decision that is time-consuming and, often, unpredictably chaotic. The <u>initial decision</u> to release the past can feel rather mechanical, whereas <u>later stages</u> are often deeply emotional. Releasing the past is not a "clean cut," not done perfectly, and will undoubtedly be met by others who offer shallow and unsolicited opinions.

Being totally transparent, the initial experience of releasing my past was an agonizing experience and, continues today. I have come to know through the teacher called 'fail' that God uses discouragement, disappointment, and loss as ways of getting my attention. And in case you have not heard, "fail" means "first attempt in learning." Some of what the reader may encounter in the pages ahead might trigger memories that have not been fully thought through. Please know there is an interrelatedness between being triggered and releasing the past. When releasing the past, a person is frequently confronted by past experiences that were thought to be neatly tucked away. I will not hide from my readers; I was triggered several times during the writing of this very chapter. Do not rush your reading. One last thought before moving forward: painful experiences in a person's life that need releasing are usually not altogether unique to them. Some people believe their painful experience is rare and that no one else can relate or understand. In short, this is a lie. *Gaining perspective on a person's past by hearing other people's stories can go a long way in "releasing the past" and living in total freedom.*

The dirty dozen signs that the past *is the present*

Below are twelve statements that are possible indicator a person's past adversely affects them today. My research on releasing the past and hours spent helping people move beyond their past helped me to create this list. If three or more of the twelve items specifically 'trigger' the reader ("That's me!"), the past may be closer than one thinks.[194] The dirty dozen list of statements provides one starting point for this study of "releasing the past". Please read through the 'dirty dozen' slowly and answer them, in your own mind, with a simple "Yes" or "No".[195]

The Dirty Dozen

1. I don't have a good relationship with myself (I have a fair amount of negative self-talk than I care to admit).
2. I do not know what happiness looks like.
3. I have a 'life used to be better' mindset.
4. I still occasionally brood over a past decision or experience.
5. I have occasional 're-runs' of (regretful) memories.
6. I am fairly certain I have an 'open door' in my life that needs to be 'closed.'
7. I think my happiness is largely dependent on some*one* or some*thing*.
8. I wish anger or being critical were not common 'go-to' emotional responses of mine.
9. I avoid thinking about a certain person or specific situation.
10. I tend to resist change.
11. I can have feelings of suspicion or mistrust regularly.
12. I have felt uncomfortable reading the 'dirty dozen.'

---

[194] If you are in a small group where you feel safe, discussing this list could be very healing. While reading, you think, "this is me", you might consider applying the 'community concept' found in an earlier chapter and seek out someone to talk with about your reading. Over the years I have heard several of these statements. And for your information, I (Bill) scored a "2" on this list. I realize on a given day my own number or score could be higher.

[195] The reader might be interested to know that our Wednesday night pilot group that went through this exact material did not get past the "dirty dozen" list. By the time we had got to this chapter in the book, people were very comfortable in sharing their stories and need for resiliency. This chapter took at least two sessions to get through.

A practical exercise for releasing the past

Seasoned counselors agree that the memory of a painful experience never entirely disappears. One writer commented, "Tears are words that need to be written down."[196] This is wise and practical counsel. When tears are accompanied by anxious thoughts, regret, confusion, apathy, or a sense of loss, writing thoughts down on paper can be very freeing. I personally do this; portions of this manuscript were written in this very way. As I begin to get out painful or confusing thoughts, ideas often come out as single words and disconnected notions. I am not concerned with structure or order in the early stages of facing an 'upset' through writing. I am more concerned with getting "out" of what is "inside" of me. John Wesley, when speaking of confessing sin, said, "Sin still remains, but no longer reigns."[197] This thought on confession can be applied to the experience of trauma. Yes, the memory of a traumatic or painful event "remains"; the experience *is* remembered. The ache *is* real. However, when the sting of the past is substantially released, the experience no longer controls or "reigns over" a person's mind and emotions. To borrow a term from the last chapter, a person can be "cut free" of the past, but ongoing support and care will still be needed. Before this chapter ends, the most important ingredient to fully releasing the past will be identified.

Before considering new material, a brief and selective recap of previously identified ideas is helpful when wanting to move forward. A released past begins when:

1) A seeker knows that resiliency is a <u>process</u> of many steps that ultimately leads to personal freedom.

2) A person learns that an experience of personal transformation can happen when least expected.

3) The journey to personal transformation begins by facing painful reality head on.

---

[196] Paulo Coelho is a Brazilian novelist with a unique style of provocative storytelling.
[197] From graduate school notes by Professor Robert Tuttle, a preeminent published Wesley scholar.

4) Triggers happen, and nearly everyone has them. Most triggers come from an
actual experience in the past that resurfaces or unexpectedly 'pops up'.

5) A 'peace (emotional stability) that passes understanding'[198] (mental clarity) is achieved when our brains experience a level of calm; a renewed life is beginning to take place.

Renewal for the wounded warrior

As I reflect on my own life, I hope my readers do not feel alone with their own unanswered and unresolved questions. I, too, have been there; greater hope and freedom can still be experienced. *Renewal for the Wounded Warrior,* written by R. Loren Sanford,[199] was a timely book for me in my own healing journey. This book made me aware that people and circumstances of my past were still holding me prisoner. I understood my painful past better when I stumbled upon the question, "What *exactly* happened?" In the early stages of my own deeper healing, I became unsure of my reality. Therefore, the question, "What *exactly* happened?" haunted me. Living between the suspected reality of a painful past and receiving personal transformation would become a process. I had trouble sleeping, invading memories from the past were commonplace. I had unresolved anger issues that needed to be confronted. The anger portion of resolving my past took years to work through. Even today, I would not say I am completely free of the memory of being the recipient of absolute wrongdoing. Risking total transparency and having never shared this before, I was told, "Bill, if you wanted to file litigation regarding _____, you'd win and would never have to work again." These words did little to absolve the depths of pain or the height of my anger. I was a mess and did not have a clue!

The "wounded warrior," says Sanford, carries both internal and external hurt. <u>Internal (emotional) wounding</u> *is harder to identify and release because it is based largely on a person's believed*

---

[198] Philippians 4. 5-7
[199] R. Loren Sanford, *Renewal for the Wounded Warrior.* (North Charleston: New Song publishers) 2010

experience. Inner pain tends to be based more on subjective experience. This truth about subjective beliefs concerning a tragic event is absolutely correct. *External wounding (events, people) tends to be more concrete or literal and, therefore easier to navigate.* Unlike inner wounding, an external event is more objective or factual. Experience has taught me external wounding is easier to process. A person strangled by their past will ask questions like, "Why?" "How was this allowed to happen?" "What about their actions that have led to my pain?" I asked ALL these questions. Sanford offers three words that are best seen as 'progressive stages', these stages or steps can help a person better frame or understand their past. Sanford uses the words, "burnout, depression and wounding." These ideas provide lasered insight as to 'why' releasing the past is difficult. Sanford's contributions are clear, based on personal experience, offer concrete 'next steps' and is not merely theory.[200]

Burnout

"Burnout" is the first 'stage' found in the life of a person with an unreconciled past. "Burnout" is seen in the corporate workforce and in relationships. "Burnout" happens when there is an *unrecognized slow depletion of mental and emotional resource*s. Burnout creeps up on an unsuspecting person and leaves one reeling and screaming, "What the ….. is happening?" Burnout is frequently found in people, like myself, who are 'first responders.' These types of people (typically ministers and counselors) want to help or meet the needs of others and begin with the purest of motives. However, along the way, these well-meaning helpers experience burnout. Because of this reality, the Apostle Paul cautions that those who are "spiritually mature" should help those in trouble *but be careful* so that the 'helper' does not fall into a similar situation.[201]

---

[200] Sanford's book was of profound importance to me, and I have read it more than once. This book should be in the office of every pastor and counselor.

[201] See Galatians 6.1f. My italics is offered as a point of emphasis. This is a serious caution by Paul that should not be missed.

"Most commonly," writes Sanford, "the origin of burnout can be traced back to performance orientation."[202] *Especially during seasons of established success*, failure to recognize that one is entering a mental and emotional 'minefield' is barely detectable. "It is entirely possible," writes Sanford, "in the glow of success or the excitement of forward motion, the warning signs of trouble are ignored."[203] When anyone lives for the adrenaline rush of success and is 'dead set' to live independently and rely on their own capabilities, this person invites disaster. Speaking very personally, I have had multiple conversations with clients where I have offered counsel and caution and, when ignored, resulted in devastation. As one enters the danger zone that I have just described, God gradually becomes less of a priority. The experience of burnout subtly happens and more commonly, than anyone cares to admit.

In his book *Fail, Finding Hope and Grace in the Midst of Ministry Failure,* J.R. Briggs describes burnout as a "slow leak". Burnout is not relegated to a colossal moral failure or an isolated poor decision but rather from the slow wearing down of the soul due to the constant drips of negativity and discouragement.[204] The lead person of an organization, educator, or home-schooling mom knows the sound of the 'constant drips of negativity' to which Briggs refers. Sanford offers his own personal reflection concerning a person who is dangerously close to burnout, "…some are so deeply depleted that they can only be carried, not exhorted and certainly not confronted…They must be loved, not instructed… during one of these times, my elders told me, 'This is our battle to fight.'"[205] I will

---

[202] R. Loren Sanford, *Healing for the Wounded Warrior.* (North Charleston: New Song publishers) 2010, pg. 5
The performance-oriented individual chooses tasks that demonstrate their abilities and avoid tasks that would make them look incompetent. This person sees failure as a sign of incompetence and therefore avoids tasks that would reveal anything that might show any personal shortcoming. Performance is seen as a means to validate a person's self-worth.

[203] Ibid., pg. 12
[204] J.R. Briggs, *Fail, Finding Hope and Grace in the Midst of Ministry Failure.* (Downers Grove: IVP Press) 2014, pg. 45
[205] R. Loren Sanford, *Healing for the Wounded Warrior.* (North Charleston: New Song publishers). Pg. 28

also say here to conclude my thoughts on burnout, when counsel and warning and loss has happened repetitively, there are some lessons in life that only the street can teach.

Depression

Sanford identifies "depression" as a second element that helps explain and better understand the pain of the past. Depression is a clinical evaluation in the mental health industry, but for our purposes here, I offer a more practical understanding is offered.[206] Prior to depression, the *slow depletion of resources* (stage one) has not been recognized. Failure to recognize the depletion of resources (stage one) *will result* in depression (stage two). Sanford comments, "Performance orientation, together with physical and emotional stress, triggers depression more than almost any other cause."[207] The remedy for depression says Sanford, "...goes much deeper than just rearranging schedules and prioritizing activities... recovery that once came about quickly, now takes a week or two before returning to feeling right again."[208]

Sanford makes a very inciteful observation about depression as it relates to those working in a church environment. Sanford distinguishes the difference between adrenaline and anointing. Sanford warns, "In the early stage (of decision making) the anointing of the Lord sustains a person in spite of fatigue... *but commonly one does not recognize the difference between the adrenaline rush and the anointing of the Lord.*"[209] Sanford later adds, "...in the early days of ministry (and I include those new to any professional setting) one neither has the wisdom or the experience to recognize the difference between anointing (presence of God) and natural strength (personal abilities)."[210]

---

[206] *The Diagnostic and Statistical Manuel for Mental Health* classifies depression as major mood disorder that is common, serious, and treatable. Those who suffer from depression experience persistent feelings of sadness and hopelessness and lose interest in activities they once enjoyed.
[207] Ibid., pg. 6
[208] Ibid., pg. 7
[209] Ibid., pg. 13; parenthesis added for clarity; italics added for emphasis
[210] Ibid., pg. 14; parenthesis added for clarity

> In 'burnout', there is an unawareness of mental and emotional depletion. In 'depression' there is an uncomfortable presence that now gnaws away and takes up residence in a person's mind.

When adrenaline replaces anointing, one part of the brain says, "Keep going" (left side of the brain) while another part of the brain (right side of the brain) says, "YOU will stop, NOW!" Having reached the "depression stage," a 'push and pull' way of life takes over. The individual who was once decisive and clear-minded now has greater difficulty with focusing and making everyday decisions. The Apostle Paul wrote of a similar mental tug of war when he wrote, "I have discovered this principle in life when I want to do what is right, I inevitably do what is wrong. I love God with all my heart, but there is another power within me that wars in my mind..."[211]

Wounding

"Wounding" is Sanford's final stage that can be applied to releasing the past. Unlike burnout where there is an *unconscious depletion of resources,* and depression where there is a *suspected possibility of an emptying of resource*s wounding has an intense awareness of personal need. Wounding therefore is, "an emotional condition, a form of stress, caused by the hurtful acts of others... the damage can be especially severe when those who we seek to serve become the cause of their pain."[212] Is there a process to releasing the depth of this pain? Yes.

First, many people that live with past pain are quite *unconscious* of this reality. An individual continues to go through life with some level of success, yet, like an iceberg, danger lurks beneath the surface. Second, a *suspected* reality that something 'not right' surfaces. Here, a person will slow down long enough to question *themselves and the world around them.* A person with a deeper deposit of wholeness or

---

[211] Romans 7.21,22 NLT
[212] Ibid, pgs. 42f.. Pages 42-57 are some of the most honest and practical information a "wounded warrior" will find.

mental clarity will talk to a trusted friend. And third, the *conscious reality* of pain is now unmistakably clear. *Conscious, painful reality is a distinct invitation from God to release the past.* Yet, during a season of pain, Sanford poses a challenging question, "What if God actually *allows* burnout, depression, and wounding to occur and be used as *tools for crucifying the flesh* and subsequently resurrecting His servants into a new life?"[213]

<u>Hard reality</u>: God uses adversity to shape people. In God's economy, nothing is wasted. Sanford comments on the reality of adversity by saying, "of rage at God can become common.... At this stage, people increasingly feel abandoned and betrayed by God. Once at this level, a person feels God has failed to keep promises and believes God is present for others but seldom for the wounded person. I know this to be absolutely true."[214] This depth of agony demands that a safe place be found to offload pain until rational thinking can be recaptured. The New Testament writer, James, offers clear counsel concerning the need for safety when healing is needed, "Therefore, confess your sins to *one another*, and pray for *one another* so that you may be healed."[215]

Referencing his own personal experience with wounding, Sanford writes, "I was backed into a corner until I had nothing else but rage. For the first time in my life, I felt driven to active hatred for certain people in my church... For my love, they returned criticism. For my best counsel, they returned distorted reflections... and to make matters worse, they enlisted other people....it left me with the bitter taste of raw emotion in my mouth. I had never consciously hated anyone before and had thought myself incapable of it. ...I cried out to God and said, "I hate these people."[216]

When a "mild upset" turns to "rage and hatred," as documented by Sanford's own admission, a person can expect to experience physical symptoms, digestive disturbances, high blood pressure, sleep disorder, prayerlessness, inability to accept help from others and the possibility

---

[213] Ibid., pg. 14. Italics added for emphasis
[214] Ibid., pg. 21
[215] James 5.16
[216] Ibid., pg. 24

of moral vulnerability and compromise. Sanford chose to "release the past, "realizing that acting out in anger would only create more stress for himself and others. Learning to separate what a person feels internally from what outward realities present is critically important. The separation of inward pain from the venomous attacks of others is virtually impossible when attempted alone. Speaking for myself, I could not do this without the help of an experienced Spirit-led counselor.

A deep wound nearly always requires a "release of the past." Releasing the past will go through the stages of <u>unconscious</u> reality to <u>suspected</u> reality to <u>conscious and undeniable</u> reality. In the "wounding" stage people struggle with personal inadequacies (despite success), feelings of guilt, anger, shame, and regret. Once acknowledging a painful reality, a person is faced with the decision to release the past. Before moving on to this critical final step that ensures the release of the past, please review the diagram below that illustrates the described healing process. I will add to this diagram in our last chapter.[217]

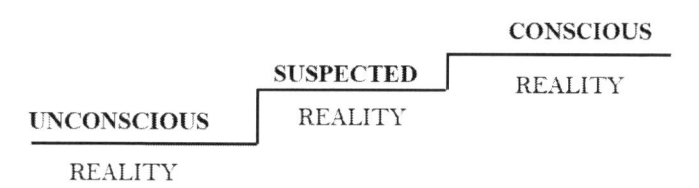

```
                                          CONSCIOUS
                       SUSPECTED          REALITY
                       REALITY
     UNCONSCIOUS
       REALITY
```

A person living with an "unconscious reality" does not know reality. Confusion rules their life, they feel 'stuck' yet, they want life to have greater meaning. This person most often, **rejects help** when it is offered. In "suspected reality" a person struggles with inadequacy because they now sense something is not right. Yet, when help is offered, the **resolutions need to be on their terms**. A person living in "conscious reality" is now **seeking help** where in earlier stages was rejecting help. Once in conscious reality, this person knows that facing the truth is THE healthiest decision they can make.

---

[217] I first developed this diagram in my book, *Out From the Shadows*. A more complete understanding of this diagram can be seen in my writing, specifically, as it relates to counselors. The diagram provided above could be a great discussion starter in a small group setting.

Forgiveness: a critical key in releasing the past

As stated from the very start, resiliency has become a hot topic if you were to do any research on your own. I have the personal conviction that to live a near fully resilient life (I am not sure anyone ever gains or 'arrives' at full resiliency), forgiveness will, at some point, play a critical role. The resilient person comes to know the benefit that forgiveness plays in living free of invasive controlling memories, thoughts, regrets, and feelings. Before going further, I want my readers to become familiar with the writings of R.T. Kendall, who I consider to be today's preeminent source on forgiveness. Kendall is right when he says, "Total forgiveness is a choice, not a feeling; at least at first, it is an act of the will."[218] Authentic forgiveness restores relationships that have been overrun by pain. When a person forgives, they trade their tired and sorry excuses for honest transparency. Gary Chapman comments in his book, *When Sorry Isn't Enough, Making Things Right With Those You Love*

> "Genuine forgiveness is a two-person transaction…the Christian is instructed to forgive others in the same manner that God forgives us. How does God forgive us? The Scriptures say that we confess our sins, and God will forgive our sins. Nothing in the Old or New Testament indicates that God forgives the sins of people who do not confess and repent of their sins."[219]

The benefits of forgiveness

When a person is caught in the vice grip of intense pain because of the actions of others, it is nearly impossible to stop and consider the benefits of accepting an apology. A hard truth must be shared here: *there are times when the admission or confession by an offending party will never come to the innocent party.* A second hard truth: a person's response to *not getting* the desired apology will reveal the emotional and spiritual health of the violated or innocent party. There

---

[218] R.T. Kendall, Total Forgiveness. (Lake Mary: Charisma House publishers, 2002), pg. 21
[219] Gary Chapman with Jennifer Thomas, *When Sorry Isn't Enough, Making Things Right With Those You Love.* (Chicago: Northfield publishing. 2013), pg.10

are certainly many benefits in what Chapman calls a "two-person transaction." Below, I offer my own short list of benefits of forgiveness. The practice of forgiveness results in:

1) A *decrease* of irrationally charged thoughts and behaviors.
2) An *increase* in peace, self-esteem, and personal empowerment.
3) A person *discovers* that forgiveness is a gift that sets them free.
4) A demonstration of forgiveness is *a supreme sign* of God's indwelling Spirit (John 20.20-22).
5) A person *learns to live in the present* and no longer dwells in the past (Isaiah 43.18)
6) And ... to NOT forgive invites the enemy to take up residence in one's life.
   (*Please consider reading* Ephesians 4. 26,27 & 2 Corinthians 2. 10,11)

The Lord's Prayer, a model prayer for forgiveness

Below is the prayer that Jesus taught his disciples (Matthew 6.1f.). Hidden in this familiar prayer is an unfamiliar outline that uniquely applies to forgiveness. I might suggest the reader read through this now and, perhaps, in a different translation.

> Our Father who art in heaven, hallowed be thy Name.
> Thy kingdom come, Thy will be done, on earth as it is in heaven.
> Give us this day our daily bread.
> And forgive us our trespasses, as we forgive those who trespass against us.
> And lead us not into temptation but deliver us from evil.
> For thine is the kingdom, and the power, and the glory,
> forever and ever.

Forgiveness begins with a "kingdom or heavenly orientation," as seen in the opening words, "our Father, who art in heaven." During the 'Jesus movement' of the 1970s, zealous young believers wore bracelets bearing the letters "WWJD," 'What would Jesus do.' Does not this same idea apply to forgiveness? To pause and ask this question could save one from experiencing even greater grief than the original offense. If a person were to pause for a moment of reflection, the heated craving for volcanic retaliation could subside. Again, releasing the past and forgiving those who have done wrong begins with having God's perspective on a situation. People might think they have very sincere and legitimate reasons for holding their beliefs about wrongdoing, but these views could be *sincerely wrong.*

True forgiveness recognizes the power of relinquishment, a turning over a person or situation to God. Authentic forgiveness does not pursue one's own version of justice. The idea of relinquishment is seen in the phrase, "Thy kingdom and Thy will be done." This phrase offered by Jesus implies NOT our way but God's way. More times than not, a person's idea of justice or 'balancing the scales' is not proportionate to the original offence. The attitude, "They need to pay," can come out in an exaggerated blistering tirade. R.T. Kendall comments about the necessity of turning a person(s) or situation over to God with these words, "The ultimate proof of total forgiveness takes place when we sincerely petition the Father to let those who have hurt us off the hook—even if they have hurt not only us but also those close to us."[220] Kendall continues to address the difficult task of releasing a person or a past situation to God when he says the greater the transgression or act of injustice against a person demands an *even greater measure* of the Spirit to help a person release and forgive those who brought abuse into one's life.[221]

Next, we find the words, "Give us this day, our daily bread". The request for "daily bread" acknowledges that to practice forgiveness, one will need to be renewed, fortified, and strengthened on a *"daily"* basis (if not moment by moment). To forgive another person is often a process that involves strenuous mental and emotional work. To recover from deep betrayal or "wounding," as described by Sanford, takes all the 'muscle' a person can muster. Therefore, a definite need to be renewed "daily" is paramount. When I use the word betrayal, I refer to the wound one receives from the hands of a person who was

---

[220] R.T. Kendall, *Total Forgiveness.* (Lake Mary: Charisma House, 2002)
[221] Ibid, pg. 76

once deeply trusted. The act of betrayal may be the deepest violation one can ever receive.[222]

The very 'heart' of the Lord's prayer highlights forgiveness, an action that has two parts: *"And forgive us… and those who have wronged us"*. The Lord's prayer is clear that forgiveness includes *confessing our sins*. John assures us, "If we confess *our sins* to him, he is faithful and just to forgive us *our sins* and to clean us from all unrighteousness."[223] But there is a second part to this prayer, "…and those who have sinned against us." I remind the reader of the familiar story of Jonah, found in the Old Testament. The beginning of Jonah's story includes God forgiving Jonah for his rebellious attitude. Later in the Jonah narrative we read God, using Jonah's voice, to stir the people of Nineveh to such a degree that revival and repentance came to this ancient city. Yet, Jonah asks God not to *forgive* the people of Nineveh. WHAT?! Jonah seems to have forgotten that God had forgiven him! I bring a most serious observation here: *there is a part of Jonah in each of us*. Part of us wants God to forgive us of our sins, shortcomings, and failures, but when it comes to those who have deeply wronged us, we do not want God to offer this same consideration. Jesus was very intentional with his instructions when talking about the subject of forgiveness. In Jesus' prayer, the master 'teacher and counselor' said our prayers should include confessing our own sins *and* that we are to forgive others.

A clear sign a person has not released a portion of their past is that closeness to God is 'interrupted' by harboring 'ill will' against an offending party. The Greek word *apheimi* translates to cancel or leave behind a debt that is owed.[224] John Bevere comments on holding onto a past offense by saying, "When an offense occurs, a debt is owed. You have heard it said, 'He'll pay for this.' So, forgiveness is like the cancellation of a debt."[225] It is common to have these thoughts. I am not permitting to have such thoughts, only saying, they commonly exist. A person does not realize that they are their own captor to the

---

[222] Concerning 'sexual betrayal' readers are directed to, *Intimate Deception, Healing the Wounds of Sexual Betrayal*, by Sheri Keffer (Grand Rapids: Revel publishers; 2019)
[223] 1 John 1.9 NLT
[224] 1 Corinthians 13.5
[225] John Bevere, *The Bait of Satan.* (Lake Mary: Charisa House. 1994)

past because the past has not been surrendered to God. The keys to the jail of the past are clenched in a person's own fists. If a person chooses not to open their hands and unlock their cell door, they will sit in a prison of their own making forever. Forgiveness is the key to the jailhouse door that leads to freedom. People who wonder why their closeness to God has vaporized do not realize their unwillingness to forgive holds them prisoner to the past. Through the intentional act of forgiveness, a person is set free from wounds caused by others. Jesus said in Luke 6. 36-38, "Judge not, and you will not be judged; condemn not, and you will not be condemned; forgive, and you will be forgiven…"

It is no coincidence the very next phrase in Jesus' prayer is, "and lead us not into temptation but deliver us from evil." What temptation was Jesus thinking of? Could it be that Jesus was thinking about the temptation that Jonah might have had? The temptation to not extend forgiveness? This phrase, "deliver us from evil," is a plea to God to keep us from the temptation of offering forgiveness in part or with conditions. A partial or conditional expression of forgiveness is not Jesus' understanding of complete forgiveness. Jesus taught that we would need to forgive often (Matthew 18. 21-22). To forgive shows us to be imitators of God (Ephesians 5. 1,2) and that to forgive is to NOT keep (or bring up) a past record of wrongs (1 Corinthians 13. 5). And of highest importance, to forgive is to outwit the very purposes and plans of the activity of Satan in our lives! (2 Corinthians 2. 10,11).

And last, Jesus' prayer comes back to the concept of "kingdom." As Jesus began his prayer with, "Our Father, who art in heaven, *thy Kingdom come...*" Jesus now closes his prayer, "For *thine is the kingdom,* and the power, and the glory, forever and ever." Jesus' prayer begins and ends with a "kingdom orientation." This concluding portion of Jesus' prayer seems to be a prayer of recommitment. The words "kingdom, power, and glory" build on one another as they reach a culminating crescendo as found in the word "glory." Once in a state that we can only imagine, stepping into God's glory positions one far, far away from the pain of any injustice that has ever been experienced.

When caught up in the beauty of God's glory, any act of injustice that has maligned a person's life will become a vapor compared to God's magnificence. I had in my office at school and now at home a plaque that reads, "Let it go." I love the message of this plaque! If a person aspires to experience God's glory here on the earth, one must "let go" of whatever a person is tethered to. Jesus' teaching of releasing the *past begins with having God's perspective.* There will be the need to petition God for *strength* to do what we humanely do not want. A person will need to be reminded that *the enemy will tempt one to not forgive.* And last, a *recommitting oneself* to God's will so that a painful past can be full, "released."

Conclusion: The gift of choice

When God created Adam and Eve, God presented them with a 'wedding gift', *the gift of choice.* They had the freedom to choose to follow God's instructions, or not. Their wrong choices cost them dearly. God gave a similar choice to Adam and Eve's son, Cain. When God asked Cain, "Why are you so angry? Why do you look so rejected? You will be accepted if you do what is right. But if you refuse to do what is right, then watch out! Sin is crouching at the door, eager to control you. You must subdue it and be its master."[226] Like his parents, Cain also, chose poorly. Deuteronomy 30:19 speaks of making Godly choices, "I have set before you life and death, blessing and cursing, therefore choose life, that both you and your descendants may live."

A third example of choice and consequence is found in Luke 23:29. This is the story of two thieves who died with Jesus. Each thief had made bad choices in their lives that resulted in a death sentence for each. One said, "If you are the Christ, save yourself." The other thief rebuked him, saying, "Do you not fear God?" Then he said to Jesus, "Remember me when You come into Your kingdom." Jesus told him, "Today, you will be with Me in paradise."[227] Three crosses: the cross of rejection, of repentance, and the center cross, the cross of redemption. From Adam and Eve to Cain to the unnamed thief on the cross, we see that God liberally offers the "gift of choice." This very same choice is offered to us.

---

[226] Genesis 3.6,7 NLT
[227] Luke 23. 42,43

Holocaust survivor Viktor Frankl once said, "Everything can be taken from a man but one thing: the last of the human freedoms — *to choose one's attitude in any given set of circumstances*, to choose one's own way." Even if a person feels like a 'leftover,' according to Jesus, nothing is wasted. John tells us that after Jesus had fed a crowd of people and they had enough to eat, Jesus instructed his disciples, "Gather the pieces that are leftover. L*et nothing be wasted.*"[228] God does not overlook anything. Even things that some people see as a "waste", matter to God. Nothing escapes the notice of God. A part of me says that God takes a certain delight in using the overlooked or the seemingly 'wasted' things in a person's life and uses these very things for His glory.

You may not feel as though your life is a "waste," but perhaps, you have feelings of insignificance. Jesus teaches, "Look at the birds of the air: they neither sow nor reap or gather in barns, and your heavenly Father feeds them. Are you not more valuable than they?[229] Paul tells us, "And we know that in all things God works for the good of those who love him, who have been called according to his purpose."[230] Not everything that happens in our lives is good, but this verse tells us that God uses our grief, our joy, our loss, our trials, and refashions everything for His purposes. God works for good, in all things. *Nothing is wasted*. And now we turn to, "Reclaiming Our Future".

<u>Resilient Realities</u>:

- o Perhaps NOTHING keeps a person from experiencing a rebooted and resilient life and then choosing to hold onto the past.
- o Releasing the past is an intentional personal decision. The <u>initial decision</u> to release the past can feel rather mechanical, whereas <u>later stages</u> can be deeply emotional.
- o Gaining perspective on the past by hearing other people's stories can go a long way in "releasing the past."

---

[228] John 6.12
[229] Matthew 6.26
[230] Romans 8. 28 NIV translation

- When a pastor of a church or the CEO of a business lives off the adrenaline rush of success and relies on their own capabilities, God gradually becomes less of a priority.
- The cycle of abuse (from the abuser) and shame (found in the innocent party) is like an emotional carrousel that continues to go around and around and getting off seems like an impossibility.
- Internal (emotional) wounding is harder to identify and release because it is based largely on a person's believed experience and not objective facts. External wounding (events) tends to be more concrete and, therefore, easier to navigate.
- Burnout does not always come because of a colossal moral failure or an isolated poor decision but from the slow wearing down of the soul due to the constant drips of negativity and discouragement.
- Conscious painful reality is an actual invitation from God to release the past.
- Learning to separate what a person feels internally from what outward realities present is critically important.
- A deep wound nearly always requires a "release of the past." Releasing the past will go through the stages of <u>unconscious</u> reality to <u>suspected</u> reality to <u>conscious and undeniable</u> reality.
- The resilient life will come to know the role and benefit that forgiveness plays in living free of invasive controlling memories, thoughts, regrets, and feelings.
- When a person experiences the vice grip of a personal and harmful at the hands of another, it is near impossible to stop and consider the benefits of offering forgiveness or accepting an apology…*if it is ever offered.*
- Forgiveness is the key to the jailhouse door that leads to freedom.

CHAPTER EIGHT

Reclaiming Your Future

"The tendency of fire is to go out, watch closely than the fire that is on the altar of your heart."

General William Booth
Founder of the Salvation Army

"...Come forth!"
Jesus; John 11.43

"There is little danger that we will take our beliefs to a fanatical extreme. Our far greater danger is that we remain content to work on a purely human level."

Wesley Duewel
Ablaze for God

Chapter Summary

- ➢ From unconscious reality to intentional resiliency
- ➢ The activation of intentional commitment to intentional resiliency
- ➢ Removing stones!
- ➢ Expressions of self-care
- ➢ Biblical basics for resiliency

Introduction

CONGRATULATIONS! You made it to the end! As we get started, please re-read the quote from William Booth at the top of the page. In speaking of the 'fire on your heart,' Booth is right to recognize that God builds a fire in a person's heart, but it is the 'responsibility of the heart' (person) to keep that fire ablaze. As you journey forward, there will be days when you will need to tend your own fire or "encourage yourself in the Lord", as David did.[231] You will need to make the intentional and disciplined effort to feed the fire in your heart that has brought you a renewed life. Self-care or self-advocating plays a

---

[231] 1 Samuel 30.6

pivotal role in "reclaiming your future". I will come back to the important life principle of self-care or self-advocacy at the end of this chapter. The third quote from revivalist Wesley Duewel is really a caution. Please re-read this, too. Some people in your life will question the new life you are experiencing and think, 'You've just gone too far.' My counsel to you is simple but critical: be careful with whom you share your deepest longings and dreams. This is important guidance to follow as you "reclaim your future."

Between the above two quotes is a reference from John's gospel that will be familiar to many readers. I will comment on this text shortly. A final word of introduction concerning the future is something I have shared previously but bears particular significance now, "To make idols of the past and rest in the security of the present are guaranteed ways to miss what the future could possibly offer." Bill Johnson comments in a similar vein as he said, "When a person's memories of the past outnumber their dreams for the future, they are beginning to die."[232]

From unconscious reality to intentional resiliency

The last chapter noted that some people *are not aware* there is a need for change in their lives. At some point, a person *suspects or slowly accepts* that something in their life *might* need to change. And finally, a person becomes very conscious that situations, relationships, and beliefs in their life need changing. To "reclaim the future" requires action. Failure to act happens partly because a person does not recognize they hold the keys to unlocking the future in their own hands! A *toxic reality seen in the lives of many believers* is the need to be in control of their own lives rather than being led by the Spirit of God. An imprisoned person has ready access to their freedom but must want to be free. This final chapter identifies and expands on the final two stages found in resilient living; these two ideas make "reclaiming the future" possible. The reader will see below the final two stages of resilient living: "intentional commitment" and "intentional resiliency." There has been a shift from "unconsciousness" to "intentionality". The regular practice of these last two stages of

---

[232] This comes from notes I had taken at a conference I attended.

spiritual growth and mental health provides sustainability in a resilient life. I stress the word "intentional" because the intentionally lived life makes deliberate choices that reflect the values and priorities that a person holds most dear. Intentionality is marked by specific, measurable goals that result in a more meaningful life and lasting joy. Please read through the illustration below and then continue in your reading …

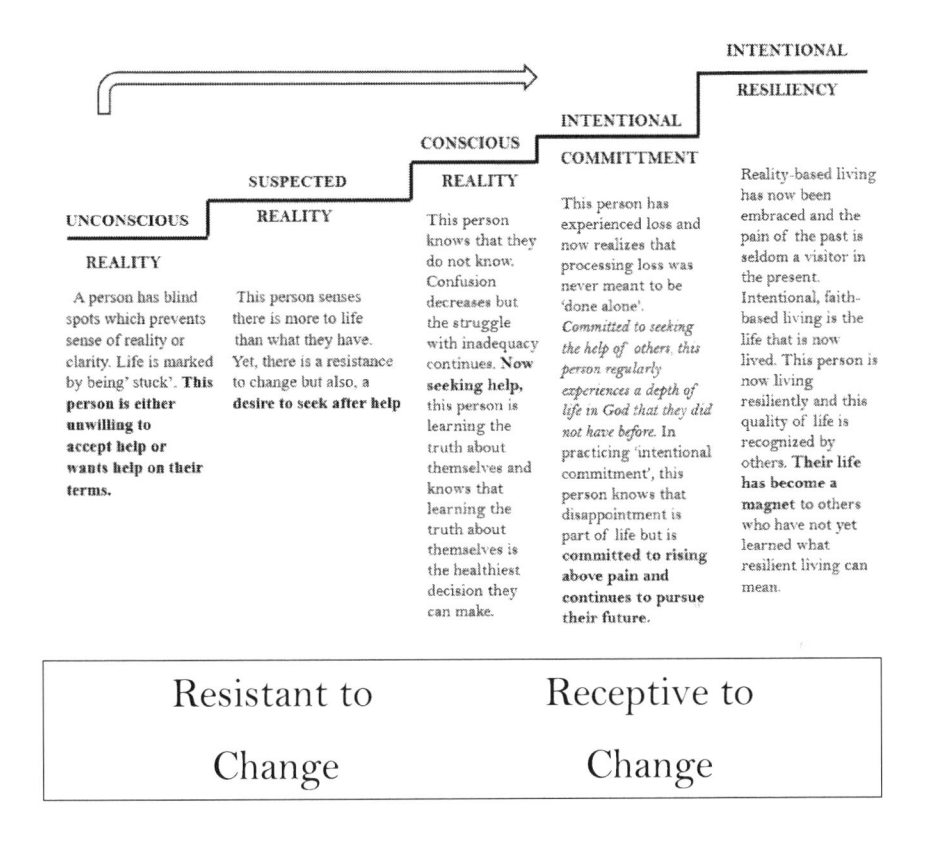

	UNCONSCIOUS REALITY	SUSPECTED REALITY	CONSCIOUS REALITY	INTENTIONAL COMMITMENT	INTENTIONAL RESILIENCY
	A person has blind spots which prevents sense of reality or clarity. Life is marked by being' stuck'. **This person is either unwilling to accept help or wants help on their terms.**	This person senses there is more to life than what they have. Yet, there is a resistance to change but also, a **desire to seek after help**	This person knows that they do not know. Confusion decreases but the struggle with inadequacy continues. **Now seeking help,** this person is learning the truth about themselves and knows that learning the truth about themselves is the healthiest decision they can make.	This person has experienced loss and now realizes that processing loss was never meant to be 'done alone'. *Committed to seeking the help of others, this person regularly experiences a depth of life in God that they did not have before.* In practicing 'intentional commitment', this person knows that disappointment is part of life but is **committed to rising above pain and continues to pursue their future.**	Reality-based living has now been embraced and the pain of the past is seldom a visitor in the present. Intentional, faith-based living is the life that is now lived. This person is now living resiliently and this quality of life is recognized by others. **Their life has become a magnet** to others who have not yet learned what resilient living can mean.

Resistant to Change	Receptive to Change

The activation of intentional commitment and intentional resiliency

The first three columns in the chart above show a *gradual* movement from unconscious reality to conscious reality. This movement does not happen overnight. Where a person once resisted help offered by others (as seen when moving from left to right) now welcomes help from mentors and caring friends[233]. A mentally and spiritually growing person knows challenges and disappointments won't kill a person, but trying to escape or ignore them just might as a person moves into the "intentional commitment" category. Specific changes have already taken place. Now, longer heard is blaming, excuse-making, victimizing, isolating from others, and minimizing difficulty. In the language of scripture, this person is rapidly becoming an "overcomer."[234] And last, "intentional resiliency" is a new way of 'doing life' and demonstrates what Jesus refers to as "abundant living."[235] Some may ask, "How long does moving through these five stages take? "It all depends on the level of desperation seen in the individual's life. The individual who is successfully "Reclaiming Their Future" knows that help from others has played a vital role in achieving resiliency. This person also realizes their newly found resiliency can be threatened at any time by a poor decision on their part or an unforeseen or unexpected life event. This leads me to reflect on one of the most beloved stories in John's gospel, a story that clearly recognizes how two sisters moved from 'blaming and resisting behaviors' to becoming the recipients of resurrected living. This story also clearly shows how an entire community became the recipients of a whole new future.

Removing stones!

The gospel writer John records that a man named Lazarus described as a dear friend of Jesus, had become sick, died, and was buried.[236] End of story ... *maybe*. In this story, the character's quality of resilience will launch an 'against all odds' reality- the reality of death. In the case of Lazarus, the first 'stone' that must be removed so a future can be claimed is the stone of *uncertainty*. One can easily imagine the sisters looking at each other with vacant stares after their brother had died as if to say, "What now?" Truly, Mary and Martha

---

[233] When I think of mentors in my life, I think of people who were both older and younger than myself. I think of people who had gifts and abilities that were very different than my own. In thinking of mentors or people of influence I also think of authors whose works are 'golden' and podcasts that I listen to, who in every sense, became my mentors although I may have never met them!
[234] John 16.33; Romans 8.37; Revelation 2.7
[235] John 10.10
[236] John 11

were facing a most uncertain life after the death of their only brother. Resilient people will not allow themselves to be hijacked by uncertainty, tragic loss, or unanswered questions.

Upon Jesus' arrival, you can hear Mary and Martha's pain, joined later by the townspeople, as they say, "If *you* had only been here...."[237] In addition to removing the stone of uncertainty, the stone of *blame* would need to be removed. This first part of John 11.32, "...if only *you*...", indicates that because the sisters were dear friends of Jesus[238], the thought of losing their only brother was beyond comprehension. *The death of their brother was Jesus' fault.* A third 'stone,' perhaps implied, but I think a possibility very much, is found in the back half of John 11.32, "...(Lazarus) would not have died". The stone I am referring to is the 'stone' of *disillusionment.* To say the sisters would have been disillusioned with Jesus because of Jesus' failure to come in a timely fashion would be a massive understatement.[239] I pause here to say being disillusioned is the result of believing an illusion. In the case of any hardship, the truly resilient person will rise above blaming or falling prey to disillusionment. It must be noted both blaming and disillusionment prevent a person from "reclaiming their future" and experiencing "abundant living."[240] I appreciate Ken Abraham's honesty when he says, "Ironically, the most dedicated Christian is a leading candidate for a spiritual mid-life crisis."[241] We do not know how spiritually mature or mentally stable Mary and Martha were but certainly they were having what any of us would experience an honest meltdown.

A fourth stone represents physical obstacles that prevent a person from "reclaiming their future." In the case of Lazarus, it was a physical stone placed in front of the grave. Examples of physical obstacles today can include the stone of poor health, dealing with an unreasonable personality at one's job, aging, a chronic complainer or

---

[237] John 11.32
[238] John 11.36: Even the 'locals' recognized how deeply Jesus felt about Lazarus
[239] Stephen W. Smith. *The Lazarus Life, Spiritual Transformation for Ordinary People.* Colorado Springs; David C. Cook 2008 Pg. 45
[240] John 10.10
[241] Ken Abraham. *The Disillusioned Christian.* San Bernardino: Here's Life publishers. 1991

the pressure of meeting a publisher's deadline. A contemporary example I can offer comes in the form of a story. I remember asking a recovering addict, "What is the biggest change you made in your recovery?" He was quick to answer, "I needed a whole new set of friends." What was he saying? He needed to "unfriend" or physically remove himself from people who were his former circle of support. Unhealthy relationships, clearly, would be an example of obstacles that need removing.

A fifth stone found in our story is perhaps the most common of all, the 'stone' of *resistance*. Resistance to change frequently is based on very rational factors. In the case of Jesus and the sisters, Jesus instructed to remove the stone in front of the grave. Yet, his instruction was met with 'resistance' as the sisters say, "… by this time there will be a bad odor, for he has been dead four days."[242] This logical objection makes sense and, many objections to change or moving forward in life will! The sisters were right; reality tells us that there would be a nasty odor coming from the grave due to the decomposing body. One clear application here is that any challenge 'covered, sealed up or entombed' challenge will have a stench when' opened.' The initial exposure of 'death' or 'death-like' behaviors in a person is not a pleasant process. Sometimes, helping a person recover their freedom can get worse before it gets better. However, resurrection power will not be denied. Resurrection power has a 'smell' of its own that overpowers the stench of death. In the case of Lazarus, Jesus came to remove the stench of death; Jesus comes today to remove smelly things in a person's life. The strength of a person's past is no obstacle to the power of God. God will move past a person's past.

Lazarus' story also introduces a most difficult final 'stone,' *having to wait on God*. Waiting on God can play an important role in "reclaiming your future." We have an advantage that Mary and Martha did not have: we know how the story eventually ends. In his book, *The Lazarus Life,* Stephen Smith says people who want an "outside-in change" in their lives are looking for a cosmetic fix. Stated another way, an immediate or superficial change is wanted, *now*. What is needed, says Smith, is an "inside-out change" that brings needed

---

[242] John 11.39

transformation.[243] Having to wait on God for an answer to any challenge provides the opportunity to think more deeply about a presenting obstacle.

Want to hear the truth? The idea of slowing down to deeply reflect on anything is very much lost in today's fast-paced culture.[244] The inability to slow down has nothing to do with age, financial means, education, or job status. The lesson of having to wait for God to act on our behalf, as found in the Lazarus story, teaches an important principle in the transformation process. Ruth Haley Barton comments on the value of waiting better than I could, "Because we do not rest (or wait) well, we lose our way... Poisoned by the hypnotic belief that good things come only through unceasing determination and tireless effort, we can never truly rest. And for want of rest, our lives are in danger."[245]

There is an uncomfortable lesson that waiting on God teaches. Waiting is extremely difficult for people who are not serious about making serious changes in their lives. Again, Steven Smith says of waiting on God, "One of the mysteries of the spiritual life is that Jesus doesn't come when we need him the most and that transformation involves a working through of our disappointments and disillusionments in life."[246] We, like Lazarus, may not be sick or close to death, but we are buried under irrational thinking, out-of-control feelings, daily routines, unresolved issues, and unanswered questions. And like the sisters, we too say, "If you had only been here...." Like Mary and Martha, we too ask, "What took you so long!?"

I offer a final thought about the idea of removing stones. As Lazarus comes out of the tomb, Jesus instructs the community to 'remove' the graveclothes that had bound Lazarus. Jesus will not do for people that which they are fully capable of doing for themselves. It is the community that releases the dead man from his grave clothes. I stress here an idea that has been communicated throughout our entire time

---

[243] Ibid., Pg. 29
[244] Ibid., Pg. 38
[245] Ruth Haley Barton. Invitation to Solitude and Silence: Experiencing God's Transforming Presence. Downers Grove: IVP 2010
[246] Ibid. Pgs. 38-39

together. As marked by trusted friendships, community is the golden thread that runs through the tapestry of spiritual freedom and ultimate resiliency.

Expressions of self-care

From the very start of this writing project, I asked myself, "How will I land this plane?" One leadership practitioner answered my question, "Begin with the end in mind'.[247] Many ideas on the care for one's own soul have been offered in our time together. As we conclude, I return to the idea of self-care again. When I personally reflect on resilient living, the idea of 'self-care' is at the top of my reflections. The idea of 'self-care' can be seen in nearly every chapter of "Resilient" and even at the very outset of this last chapter! I intentionally chose to close our time by looking at how David, one of my favorite biblical characters, practiced "self-care."

David was no stranger to trouble and would need to learn how to navigate extremely difficult challenges In a look at David's life, we see a shepherd to sheep during his youth, a brother amongst brothers in his earlier years, a musician before a paranoid king, and an unlikely military hero at a very young age. David could defeat the giant Goliath, but not the giant of his passions. He survived multiple murder attempts by jealous King Saul. David was described as a "man after God's own heart,"[248] yet his earthly family was in disarray. The scene of David on his deathbed doesn't portray a devoted family gathered at his bedside. Rather, Adonijah, David's oldest son, is seen making plans to make himself king rather than being concerned about his dying father.[249] My heart and mind leads me to believe that David often processed deep thoughts and feelings *alone*. Only his faithful God could fully understand the complexities of both his heart and

---

[247] Stephen Covey. *7 Habits of Highly Effective People.* Simon and Shuster. New York City: Simon and Schuster. 2020
[248] 1 Samuel 13.14
[249] 1 Kings 1. This story ends tragically as Adonijah, the fourth son of King David, described as very handsome (1 Kings 1.6) schemes to take the throne away from Solomon, who was now King. When Solomon learns of this political coo by his half-brother, he orders the execution of Adonijah that very day (1 Kings 2. 23-25).

mind. Over time, David learned to encourage himself in the Lord, as if there was no one else or no other place for him to go.[250]

Psalm 42 offers very practical self-care principles. The psalm begins

> As the deer pants for the water brooks, So my soul pants for You, O God. My soul thirsts for God, for the living God; When shall I come and appear before God?[251]

These opening two verses harken back to David's days as a shepherd boy, seeing a thirsty deer in a barren wilderness longing for a cool stream. David is saying he is the deer that "pants" for the Lord. David expresses a similar idea in another psalm as he writes, "I opened my mouth wide and panted, for I longed for Your commandments."[252] The remainder of Psalm 42 offers clear self-care guidance to any heart that longs for resilient living. The first self-care principle for a resilient life is having *desperation*. As stated earlier, 'desperate desperation' propels a person from "unconscious reality" to "intentional resiliency." Little desperation equals little growth. Greater desperation results in greater (and perhaps faster?) growth. This is not a prescription by any means but only one description of growth.

A second self-care principle is the practice of *"emotional transparency"*. We see this in reference to "tears" in verses three and again in verse 10. David writes, "My bones suffer mortal agony as my foes taunt me, saying to me all day long, 'Where is your God?'"[253] This self-care principle is perhaps only attained through great difficulty. Rachel Hollis, in her book *I Didn't See That Coming*, offers very practical counsel, "…when facing unforeseen challenges and moving forward in spite of them, you must decide that there is something greater at stake than the way you're feeling or your fear of ever feeling pain, again." [254] "Emotional transparency" is not passive in nature. The activity of emotional transparency can play a significant

---

[250] Psalms 52, 91 and 103 are all seen to be writings of David that clearly show a heart turned towards God.
[251] Psalms 42. 1,2
[252] Psalms 119. 131, 132
[253] Psalms 42.10
[254] Rachel Hollis. *Didn't See That Coming: Putting Life Back Together*. Harper Collins. 2020

role in a person's ability to live resiliently. When I think of emotional transparency, I think in terms of authenticity. God can handle our authentic, gritty, gutsy, and emotionally charged laments, as seen in the life of David. Job is another biblical character who was authentic before God. In Job 42, God speaks approvingly of the times when Job openly and honestly let God know of his displeasure with his God. God refers to Job's painful cries as "truthful"[255] communion. Job's 'truthful communion' with Creator God is contrasted to Job's three friends as God says to Eliphaz, Bildad, and Shuhite, "I am angry with you because you have not spoken the truth about me as has my servant Job."[256] Authenticity displays honesty, vulnerability, and results in increased discernment. Such dogged authenticity will safeguard a person against moral, mental, or emotional shortcomings.

A third spiritual self-care practice is found in verse four, "These things I remember as I pour out my soul: how I used to go to the house of God under the protection of the Mighty One with shouts of joy and praise among the festive throng." This verse exemplifies the practice of *spiritual self-talk.* Spiritual self-talk is developed by "pouring out" one's soul to God, going to the "house of God," affirming the sufficiency of God, and through the spiritual discipline of worship as seen in "shouts of joy and praise."

A fourth spiritual self-care practice is found in verse five, "Why are you so downcast, O my soul, and why are you in turmoil within me? Hope in God; for I shall again praise him, my salvation and my God." This verse exemplifies the embrace of one's *emotional reality. Please note*, when reading through *the entirety of this psalm*, there is the ongoing reality of adversity and pain, yet the writer continues to come back to the greater reality of the active presence and never forgotten promises of his God. God's presence is always the antidote to human

suffering. And God's promises are the fuel that keeps the fire in one's heart burning. R.C. Sproul was fond of saying, "I always do not feel the presence of God. But, God's promises are not based upon my feelings but God's integrity."

---

[255] Job 42. 6,7
[256] Job 42. 6

A fifth and final spiritual self-care principle to not lose sight of is one's *focus on God*. In Psalm 42. 5, David writes, "For I shall again praise him, my salvation and my God.." And again, in verse 8, we read, "By day the Lord commands his steadfast love, and at night his song is with me, a prayer to the God of my life." You may read this fifth self-care principle and think, "Focus on God? This sounds so…basic. I remind the reader that God often brings us back to the basics, especially during times of conflict, as was the case with David. God said to the church at Ephesus, "*Go back* and do the things *you did at first.*"[257]

Biblical basics for resilient living

For centuries, a segment of biblical scholarship has written and compiled volumes of research on what is called 'systematic theology.'[258] This branch of scholarship seeks to summarize specific biblical ideas, such as reason and revelation, various doctrines, the character and personhood of God, Christian ethics, and the mission of the Church, to name a few. A systematic approach to matters concerning faith and practice empowers and helps believers know how to live their lives in Christ.

As I conclude, I offer "biblical basics" that are foundation stones that *specifically relate to the resilient life*. Without holding to these basics, the practice of resiliency will be near impossible.

The resilient life recognizes that….

- God is love (1 John 4.7). In every incomprehensible life circumstance, good or tragic, God seeks to make Himself known through unconditional and extravagant caregiving of all people. When He showed His glory to Moses, God revealed Himself as "the compassionate and gracious God, slow to anger, abounding in love and faithfulness, maintaining love to

---

[257] Revelation 2.5
[258] John Calvin's, *The Institutes of the Christian Religion*, published in 1536, is considered by many to be a pillar example of systematic theology. Modern or more current compilations of systematic theology today are offered by Wayne Grudem, Stanley Grentz and Wolhart Pannenburg.

thousands, and forgiving wickedness, rebellion and sin" (Exodus 34:6-7, NIV).

- God is good (Mark 10.18; 1 Timothy 4.4), and because of this, God can be trusted. God's presence is a refuge in times of trouble (Nahum 1.7).
- Scripture alone is the final and sufficient authority for life and decision-making. God's word revealed in both the Old and New Testament is sufficient for faith and practice (2 Timothy 3:16-17).
- By nature, people are slaves to sin, but Jesus came to set prisoners free (John 8.31f; Isaiah 61)
- Failure to recognize the depth of depravity in one's own life diminishes a person's willingness and ability to offer grace to others (Jonah 4.1f; Titus 3. 3-5).
- Addressing the needs of others is commanded by Jesus and in like manner, the resilient life seeks to deeply care for all people. *(Matthew 25. 35-36)*
- Being rejected is a reality of life but not a reflection of a person's worth. Rejection can be God's way of redirecting a person to something better. "He was despised and rejected by mankind, a man of suffering, and familiar with pain. Like one from whom people hid their faces; he was despised, and we held him in low esteem" (Isaiah 53.3).
- The rebooted and resilient life means a person has become a new creation in Christ, the old life has passed away, and new adventures await. (2 Corinthians 5.17)
- Authentic signs of a rebooted life include being filled with the Holy Spirit as demonstrated by the display of fruit (Galatians 5), character (Matthew 5), gifting (Ephesians 4; Romans 12; 1 Corinthians 12), a readiness to forgive (John 20) and the desire to share the Good News of the Gospel (Matthew 28. 18f.; Acts 2)
- The centrality of the cross. Christ suffered and died for all humanity. There will be times that God asks His people to push through times of their own personal suffering (2 Timothy 2.3;

1 Thessalonians 3.4) and recognize and join in with the sufferings of others (Romans 12.15; 2 Corinthians 1. 3-6).

- The "chief end of man" or humanity's 'twin goals' (taken for the Westminster Shorter Catechism, 1646[259]) is to glorify God and enjoy him forever. God's heartfelt desire for every believer is to have a relationship with God that would be enjoyed in every season of life.

Resilient Realities

- o You will need to make the intentional and disciplined effort to feed the fire in your
  heart that has brought you a renewed life.
- o An imprisoned person has ready access to their own freedom, but they must want
  to be free.
- o A mentally and spiritually growing person accepts that challenges and disappointments won't kill a person, but trying to escape or ignore them just might.
- o Resilient people will not allow themselves to be hijacked by uncertainty or unanswered questions.
- o Waiting, especially if it is lengthy, cannot be practiced by people who are not serious about making serious changes in their lives.
- o We, like Lazarus, maybe a little sick and not yet dead, but we are buried under disconnected thoughts, feelings, daily routines, unresolved issues, and unanswered questions.
- o Jesus will not do for people that which they are fully capable of doing for themselves.
- o Little desperation equals little growth, whereas greater desperation results in greater growth. This is not a prescription by any means but only one description of growth.

---

[259] *The Westminster Shorter Catechism* is a historic and still helpful summary of core beliefs and doctrines. This document, in the past, was used as a teaching tool with younger children, to guide them in their beliefs and how they might live. live.

- "…when facing unforeseen challenges and moving forward in spite of them, you must decide that there is something greater at stake than the way you're feeling or your fear of ever feeling pain again."
- Authenticity displays the needed transparent character traits of honesty, vulnerability, and discernment that safeguard a person against moral, mental, or emotional shortcomings.
- As marked by trusted friendships, community is the golden thread that runs through the tapestry of spiritual freedom and ultimate resiliency.

A Final Word: "Suddenly"

It was late when I got home from our small group last night. For ten weeks, we discussed excerpts from "Resilient." Our group, ranging between twenty to twenty-five adults in attendance, was a mixture of ages, personal backgrounds, and faith experiences. This very diverse group had an equal number of men and women. Now living in Chattanooga, Tennessee, participants were transplants from New York, New York to San Diego, California, and many points between. As was his custom, Greg began our evening with a question,

> "When you were young, what did you want to be when you grew up?"

The answers included being a meteorologist, an actress, an astronaut, a momma, a cowboy, a doctor, and many more. To my knowledge, except for becoming a "momma," no one became what they had once imagined.

Resilient presupposes having had a disappointment. Resilience is the ability to withstand adversity without being consumed by disappointment. Like a child whose hoped-for dream did not come to pass or an adult who fails to achieve a desired goal, the resilient person will not allow frustration or regret to discourage them. I am reminded of the scriptural maxim, "…where there is no vision, people perish."[260] Such is the case with resiliency; if a person doesn't have the vision to 'get up again' after a hardship, life most assuredly becomes much more difficult.

Failure is *underrated*. Some of the most significant recorded achievements followed failure. Here are but a few examples:

- George Washington lost two-thirds of all the battles he fought but is credited with winning the Revolutionary War and later became the first U.S. president.
- Abraham Lincoln had six political defeats before being elected the 16th president of the United States.
- Napoleon graduated 42nd in a class of 43.

---

[260] Proverbs 29.18

- In 21 years, Babe Ruth hit 714 home runs and struck out 1,330 times. He struck out nearly twice as often as he hit a home run.
- Thomas Edison reported 1,000 failed attempts before creating the first light bulb.
- Henry Ford's first two automobile companies failed.
- Elvis Presley was ordered off the Grand Old Opry stage.
- Michael Jordon was cut from his high school basketball team.
- A Hollywood producer described Fred Astaire in the following way: "Can't act. Slightly bald and can dance a little."

In his best-selling book, *Failing Forward*, John Maxwell comments, "The difference between average people and achieving people is their perception of and response to failure."[261] I also read recently, "If you want to succeed, plan to fail."[262] And I add to Maxwell's equation for achievement: learn to become resilient.

I offer a final "resilient reality" taken from the twenty-fourth chapter of Luke's gospel; this solitary word is "suddenly." Following the death and resurrection of Jesus, two men make the seven-mile trek from Jerusalem to a town of Emmaus. Luke tells us Jesus joins them "suddenly." The word 'suddenly' is important to Luke, and he uses it frequently in his writing. Luke tells his readers these men had walked with Jesus, talked with him as they traveled, and shared a common meal but were kept from recognizing him. Then over a meal, conversations that were once only heard were *suddenly* translated into the recognizable person of Jesus; confusion turns to unexplainable excitement. There is a lesson in resilience here: *resilient living can happen "suddenly."* What is it that keeps people from recognizing, much less accepting, help? Why can some people *suddenly* make mid-course life changes while others simply cannot? Certainly, there are many factors to answering this question, but I offer here this promise-*the resilient life is available to anyone*. Jesus once taught,

"If God gives such attention to the appearance of wildflowers—most of which are never even seen—don't you think he'll attend to you, take pride in you, do his best for ou? What I'm trying to do here is to

---

[261] Maxwell, John. *Failing Forward*. (Nashville: Thomas Nelson books. 2000. Pg. 2)
[262] Craig Groschel in a recent (1/2024) podcast newsletter

get you to relax, to not be so preoccupied with *getting*, so you can respond to God's *giving*. People who don't know God and the way he works fuss over these things, but you know both God and how he works. *Steep your life in God-reality, God-initiative, God-provisions. Don't worry about missing out. You'll find all your everyday human concerns will be met.* Give your entire attention to what God is doing right now, and don't get worked up about what may or may not happen tomorrow. God will help you deal with whatever hard things come up when the time comes."[263]

A 'sudden experience' of any kind can ignite the desire to get up one more time; new priorities and purpose will be discovered. <u>Hard truth</u>: when a person is not accustomed to living with "suddenly" and a "suddenly" experience happens, a person feels very vulnerable.

C. S. Lewis, in his tale, *The Lion, the Witch, and the Wardrobe*[264], tells of four children, Peter, Susan, Edmund, and Lucy, who set out to explore the strange and somewhat frightening country of Narnia, a realm locked under evil's spell. Lewis explains that Narnia is ultimately ruled by a benevolent Presence, a lion named Aslan.[265] One day, Lucy and Susan come upon Mr. and Mrs. Beaver, who assure the girls that Aslan is about to set things right and destroy evil's plans. Concerning Aslan, Lucy asks, "Is—is he a man?" Mr. Beaver, rather sternly, says, "Aslan, a man? Certainly not. I tell you, he is the King of the wood…Don't you know who is the King of Beasts? Aslan is a lion—the lion, the great Lion."

"Ooh!" said Susan, "I'd thought he was a man. Is he…safe? I shall feel rather nervous about meeting a lion." In her calming voice, Mrs. Beaver says, "Make no mistake, if there's anyone who can appear before Aslan without their knees knocking, they're either braver than most or else just silly." Still feeling quite unsure of herself, Lucy needs clarification and asks, "Then…he isn't safe, is he?" Now, looking straightaway into Lucy's frightened eyes, Mr. Beaver offers these

---

[263] Matthew 6. 30-34, The Message translation. Italics added for emphasis
[264] Lewis, C.S. *The Lion, the Witch, and the Wardrobe.* (New York: Collier books. 1950, pages. 74,75)
[265] I stop here to observe the co-existence of evil and promise of deliverance as seen in Narnia, is not imaginary in our culture and is seen in our very real culture.

words, "Safe? Who said anything about safe? Of course, he isn't safe. *But he's good, I tell you…*"

I have experienced many exhilarating and life-changing "suddenlies" in my lifetime and missed far more; of this, I am sure. I have written *Resilient* because I, like the children in the *Chronicles of Narnia* tale, once felt nervous when initially experiencing the presence of God. But today, I seek and welcome God's healing presence. The God I have met on my life's journey has been more than "safe." And, as Mr. Beaver said, and I now know, God is good. Similarly, like the men on their journey in Luke's travelogue, God "suddenly" appeared to me many times as I wrote. I pray the same can become true for you, too.

Today, I no longer want to keep my "sudden stories" to myself. I know living a resilient life requires a transparent lifestyle. In writing these final thoughts, I was reminded of a biblical text found in the last book of the bible, the book of Revelation. This text says, now salvation and power has come. The one who once brought accusation and sought to align believers has been ultimately defeated. The defeat was made possible by the blood of the Lamb and the confident words of their testimony that they readily share with all to hear.[266]

During my writing I learned the importance of slowing down, risk, letting go of things I could not control, sharing 'stuff' with a trusted friend, resisting negativity, 'taking the higher road' even when I felt I was being taken advantage of, and removing the mask of pretense and falsehood. Because the one who once accused me has been defeated, I feel a liberation and obligation to share the stories of my life with much greater freedom. I interpret Jesus' final words on the cross, "It is finished" as a personal charge of a new beginning, to me. The resilient life is far, far more than gaining information, reading a book, being in a small group or saying a prayer. The resilient life is best understood to be a constant unfolding that results in total transformation, but a price must be paid.

Early in my career, as speaking invitations became more frequent, I overheard an older leader say about me, "He just dreams too big a dream." There is a word for this jealous comment, 'curse.' You know from what I have shared with you that I have experienced my own share of injustices. With each one, I had a choice to make. The

---

[266] I wrote my own translation of Revelation 12. 10,11

resilient life makes the choice to 'get up after life knocks a person down.' *Resilient* was never intended to be a book to be read but rather, a mirror to help readers see themselves more clearly. Look for your next "suddenly". It may be just around the corner; step into it, and you may discover a life waiting for you that you have never before experienced.

Oh, thank you for taking this journey with me. I truly hope our paths one day, 'suddenly' connect.... Until then, catch me on "Open Door" podcast (seen on Facebook, Spotify and other social media platforms).

Author's Favorite Resilient Realities

"Crucified, laid behind a stone
You lived to die, rejected and alone
Like a rose, trampled on the ground
You took the fall and thought of me,
Above all"[267]

- Without change there can be no breakthrough and without a breakthrough, there can be no future.
- If a person can harness the power that resiliency unleashes, there is no limit to what a person can accomplish.
- A hard truth about trying to help a person who has a victim mentality is that some people prefer victimization over liberation.
- People will believe in you before they believe in your God. If people in pain are not assured that the person offering help is deeply invested in their pain, game over.
- Pain is the chisel in the toolbox of the Master Craftsman and is often the most common tool used that leads to God's transforming power.
- If a person is to experience authentic community, one must risk.
- Community can be the midwife that 'delivers' a person's future.
- Idols of the past, and a holding onto the security of the present, are guaranteed ways to miss what the future could offer.
- It is easy to know facts and miss truth.
- The cycle of abuse (from an abuser) and shame (entrenched in the innocent party) results in an emotional carrousel that continues to go around and around; getting off seems like an impossibility.
- Conscious painful reality is an actual invitation from God to release the past.

---

[267] Smith, Michael W. *Above All*. Originally written by Lenny Leblanc and Paul Baloche; recorded in 1995

- Forgiveness is the key to the jailhouse door that leads to freedom.
- Jesus will not do for people that which they are fully capable of doing for themselves.
- "…when facing unforeseen challenges and movement forward in spite of them, one must decide there is something greater at stake than present feelings or fear of ever feeling pain, again."
- Authenticity displays the needed transparent character traits of honesty, vulnerability, and discernment. These qualities, found in authenticity, safeguard a person against moral, mental or emotional shortcomings.
- Community, marked by trusted friendships, is the golden thread that runs through the tapestry of spiritual freedom and ultimate resiliency.
- *Resilient* was never intended to be a book to be read but rather, a mirror used by readers see themselves more clearly.

Bibliography

Abraham, Ken. *The Disillusioned Christian.* (San Bernardino: Here's Life publishers. 1991)
Allender, Dan & Loerzel, Cathy. *Redeeming Heartache, How Past Suffering Reveals
Our True Calling.* (Grand Rapids: Zondervan publishing. 2021)
Arterburn, Stephen. *Healing is a Choice.* (Nashville: Thomas Nelson books, 2004)
Addicted to Love (Ann Arbor: Servant Publications. 1991)
Barton, Ruth Haley. Invitation to Solitude and Silence:
Experiencing God's Transforming Presence.
(Downers Grove: Intervarsity Press)
Strengthening the Soul of Your Leadership. (Downers Grove: IVP press, 2008)
Beumer, Jurgen. Henri Nouwen, A Restless Seeking for God. (New York: Crossroad books. 1997)
Bevere, John. *The Bait of Satan.* (Lake Mary: Charisa House, 1994)
Briggs, J.R. *Fail, Finding Hope and Grace in the Midst of Ministry Failure.* (Downers Grove: IVP Press, 2014)
Brown, Brene'. *Daring Greatly.* (New York: Penguin books, 2012)
The Gifts of Imperfection. (Center City: Hazeldon publishing, 2010)
Rich Buhler, *Pain and Pretending*, (Nashville: Thomas Nelson books, 1991, revised in 1998,
IVP 2010)
Chapman, Gary with Jennifer Thomas, *When Sorry Isn't Enough, Making Things Right With
Those You Love.* (Chicago: Northfield publishing, 2013)
Chapman Gary. *Rising Above a Toxic Workplace* (Chicago: Northfield publishing, 2014)
Cloud, Henry. *Necessary Endings.* (New York: Harper Collins publishing, 2010)
Cloud, Henry and John Townsend. *How People Grow.* (Grand Rapids: Zondervan. 2001)
Colbert, Don. *Deadly Emotions.* (Nashville: Thomas Nelson publishers. 2003)
Covey, Stephen. *7 Habits of Highly Effective People.* (New York City: Simon and Schuster, 2020)
De Silva, Dawna. *Shifting Atmosphere, Discerning and Displacing the Spiritual Forces Around You*

(Shippensburg: Destiny Image books, 2017)
Effler, Bill. *Out From the Shadows, Biblical Counseling Revealed in the Story of Creation.*
(Bloomington: Westbow Press, 2014)
Enroth Ronald. *Churches That Abuse* (Grand Rapids: Zondervan publishing, 1992)
Frankl, Viktor, *Man's Search for Meaning*, Beacon Press, 1947 (first printing)
Craig Groeschel, *The Christian Atheist, Believing in God but Living as if He Doesn't Exist.*
(Grand Rapids: Zondervan, 2011).
Hollis, Rachel. *Didn't See That Coming: Putting Life Back Together.* (New York: Harper Collins. 2020)
Jennings, Timothy. *The God Shaped Brain.* (Downers Grove: Baker books, 2013)
Jobe, Mark. *UNSTUCK, Out of Your Cave and Into Your Call.* (Chicago: Moody Press, 2014)
Keffer, Sheri. *Intimate Deception, Healing the Wounds of Sexual Betrayal*, by Sheri Keffer
(Grand Rapids: Revel publishers; 2018)
Kendall, R.T. *The Parables of Jesus: A Guide to Understanding and Applying the Stories Jesus Told*
(Grand Rapids: Baker Books, 2008)
Total Forgiveness. (Lake Mary: Charisma House publishers, 2002)
Kinnaman, David. *You Lost Me, Why Young Christians Are Leaving Church.*
(Grand Rapids: Baker Books, 2011
Unchristian, What a new generation really thinks of Christianity.
(Grand Rapids, Baker Books, 2007)
Kollar, Charles Allen. *Solution Focused Pastoral Counseling.* (Grand Rapids: Zondervan, 1997)
Kruger, Michael J., *Bully Pulpit, Confronting the Problem of Spiritual Abuse in the Church.*
(Grand Rapids: Zondervan reflective. 2023)
Kraus, John R., *Quick Scripture Reference for Counseling.* (Grand Rapids: Baker Books, 1994)
Leaf, Caroline. *Cleaning Up Your Mental Mess.* (Grand Rapids: Baker Books, 2023)
Who Switched Off My Brain? (Dallas: Thomas Nelson, 2007)
Lewis, C.S. *A Grief Observed* (New York: Bantam, 1961)

The Problem of Pain (New York: HarperCollins, 1940/1996)

The Lion, the Witch and the Wardrobe, Chronicles of Narnia series (New York: Collier books, 1950)

Lewis, J. Kirk and Melanie. *Desperate Dependency*. (Enumclaw: WinePress publishing. 2011)

Manning, Brennan. *The Ragamuffin Gospel*. (Colorado Springs: Multnomah Books, 1990)

Middleton-Moz, Jane. *Masters of Disguise, Shame and Guilt*. (Deerfield Beach: Health Communications, Inc. 1990)

Lotz, Anne Graham. *Wounded by God's People*. (Grand Rapids: Zondervan publishers, 2013)

McNutt, Judith. *Angels Are For Real*. (Bloomington: Chosen Books, 2012).

Merton, Thomas. *Merton's Place of the Heart* (Notre Dame: Ave Maria Press, 1978)

Nieuwhof, Carey. *Didn't See It Coming*. (Colorado Springs: Waterbook Pres. 2018)

Nouwen, *In the Name of Jesus*, (New York: Crossroad Books, 1999)

The Road to Daybreak. (New York: Image books, 1988 (first publication)

The Inner Voice of Love, (New York: Image Books, 1996)

The Wounded Healer. (New York: Doubleday Books, 1972)

The Return of the Prodigal, (New York: Doubleday books, 1994)

Omaritan, Stormie. *Lord, I Want To Be Whole*, (Nashville: Thomas Nelson publishers, 2000)

Reese, Andy. *Freedom Tools, Overcoming Life's Problems*. (Grand Rapids: Chosen Book, 2008)

Sanford, R. Loren. *Renewal for the Wounded Warrior*. (North Charleston: New Song publishers, 2010)

Seamands, David. *Healing of Memories* (Wheaton: Victor books, 1985)

Stanley, Andy. *Enemies of the Heart*. (Colorado Springs: Multnomah Press. 2006)

Smith, Stephen W. *The Lazarus Life, Spiritual Transformation for Ordinary People.*
(Colorado Springs; David C. Cook, 2008)

TerKeurst, Lysa. *It's Not Supposed To Be This Way: Finding Unexpected Strength When Disappointment Leaves You Shattered,* (Nashville: Thomas Nelson publishers, 2018)

Uninvited, Living Loved When You Feel Less Than, Left Out and Lonely.
(Nashville; Thomas Nelson publishers. 2016)
Van Der Kolk, Bessel. *The Body Keeps the Score: Brain, Mind and Body in the Healing of Trauma*
(New York: Penguin Books, 2014)
Wilder, Jim and Michel Hendricks. *The Other Half of Church.* (Chicago: Moody Press, 2020)
Wilder, Jim and Ray Woolridge, *Escaping Enemy Mode.* (Chicago: Northfield publishing, 2023)
Wilkinson, Bruce. *The Dream Giver*, (Colorado Springs: Multnomah Books, 2003)

Author Description

A native Californian, Dr. Bill Effler received his undergraduate degree from the *University of Southern California* and two postgraduate degrees from *Fuller Theological Seminary* (MDiv. and DMin., with a concentration on leadership and mental health). As an ordained Presbyterian pastor (PCUSA), he held staff positions in four churches, including that of Senior Pastor. In other professional venues he has been an intake counselor in a residential treatment facility, a case counselor in a group practice, and consults with churches and businesses in the non-profit sector, including the Southeastern Tennessee *Alzheimer's Association* where he was a board member and *Living Free*, where he currently serves as an advisory board member to the president. From 2000 to 2023 he was on the faculty in the School of Theology and Ministry at *Lee University*, in Cleveland, Tennessee, where he taught a wide range of courses in the pastoral studies arena, including senior level classes, *Pastoral Counseling* and *Gender and Spirituality.* Dr. Effler also served in the university's *Center for Calling and Career*.

While serving a local church in the San Francisco Bay Area at the early outset of the HIV/Aids epidemic, Bill became emersed in counseling, particularly in the homosexual community. Throughout his entire career as pastor, educator or counselor, engaging people in deep pain has been a focus of his personal, professional, and academic life. His podcast, *Open Door* was released in January 2020 with over 7000 views before the COVID crises hit in March. He addressed such topics as, "The Boy Crises", "The Girl Crises", "The Message of the LGBTQ Community" and, "A Conversation with Andy Negra, Experiencing the Battle of the Bulge". With the release of "Resilient", *Open Door* will start to air again and can be found on a variety of social media platforms.

Previously published works include, *Turning the Church Inside Out, Mission of the Church: Practical Theology for the Twenty-First Century* where he acted as General Editor and contributor and, *Out From the Shadows, Biblical Counseling Revealed in the Story of Creation.*

He and his wife, Kristen, reside in Apison, Tennessee and are the parents of three grown children. Today Bill is on staff, part time, as a counselor at the *Transformation Center*. When not counseling Bill can be found herding his chickens, gardening, doing research and writing. Dr. Effler can be reached at weffler@leeuniversity.com,

Made in the USA
Columbia, SC
04 April 2024